D0962822

eDonato, Collete.
ity of one : young
riters speak to the wor
2004.
3305208300735
a   04/15/05

City of One
Young Writers Speak to the World

From WritersCorps

Foreword by Isabel Allende
Edited by Colette DeDonato

SANTA CLARA COUNTY LIBRARY

3 3305 20830 0735

published by Aunt Lute Books, San Francisco

Copyright © 2004 WritersCorps, San Francisco, a project of the San Francisco
Arts Commission

Foreword © 2004 Isabel Allende

All rights reserved. This book, or parts thereof, must not be used or reproduced in
any form whatsoever without written permission from the publisher.

First Edition
10-9-8-7-6-5-4-3-2-1

Aunt Lute Books
P.O. Box 410687
San Francisco, CA 94141

Photo credit: Mission Girls © 2004 WritersCorps, San Francisco
Cover and Text Design: Amy Woloszyn

Executive Director: Joan Pinkvoss
Artistic Director: Shay Brawn
Managing Editor: Gina Gemello
Marketing Director: Marielle Gomez
Production: Stacey Caro, Shahara Godfrey

This book was made possible in part by grants from the Isabel Allende Foundation;
the LEF Foundation; the Miranda Lux Foundation; the Richard and Rhoda
Goldman Fund; the San Francisco Foundation; San Francisco Mayor's Department
of Children, Youth and Family; the Department of Juvenile Probation; the Youth
Arts Fund; and the National Endowment for the Arts.

ISBN 1-879960-69-9

Library of Congress Cataloging-in-Publication Data

City of one : young writers speak to the world / from WritersCorps ; edited by
Colette DeDonato ; foreword by Isabel Allende.
    p. cm.
    ISBN 1-879960-69-9 (pbk. : alk. paper)
1. Youths' writings, American—California—San Francisco. 2. Immigrants'
writings, American—California—San Francisco. 3. Youths' writings, American—
New York (State)—New York. 4. Immigrants' writings, American—New York
(State)—New York. 5. Youths' writings, American—Washington (D.C.)
6. Immigrants' writings, American—Washington (D.C.) 7. American poetry—21st
century. 8. Children of immigrants—Poetry. 9. Immigrants—Poetry. 10. Youth—
Poetry. I. DeDonato, Colette. II. WritersCorps.

PS508.Y68C57 2004
810.8'09283—dc22

                                                            2004045089

Acknowledgments

WritersCorps would like to acknowledge our editor Colette DeDonato for her vision of this book and keen ability to transform hundreds of submissions into a work of art. A talented writer and former teacher in WritersCorps, Colette was the perfect editor for the job and approached the work with great spirit. Her insights as a teacher, writer, and thinker make *City of One* one of the most powerful collections published by WritersCorps.

WritersCorps would also like to thank Valerie Chow Bush, former WritersCorps Publications Coordinator, for her sage advice and for the WritersCorps books she edited during her tenure (1999-2002): *What It Took for Me to Get Here, Smart Mouth, Jump,* and *Believe Me, I Know.* Thanks to Judith Tannenbaum, Training Coordinator, and WritersCorps teachers Mahru Elahi, Jime Salcedo-Malo, Beto Palomar and Chad Sweeney for reading and editing the manuscript and helping shape the book. Thanks to Sierra Filucci for typing the submissions and laying the early groundwork for the book. Thanks to Green Gulch Farm Zen Center for allowing WritersCorps to conduct a writing workshop in the peace garden. Thanks to Isabel Allende and Lori Barra from the Isabel Allende Foundation. Without Isabel's support, we would not have embarked on such an important project.

None of the writing in this book would have come about if not for the dedicated writers who taught in our program and inspired their students to take the risk and write.

1994-2004 WritersCorps Teachers (San Francisco)
Cathy Arellano, Ellis Avery, Alegria Barclay, Stephen Beachy, Cherie Bombadier, Godhuli Bose, Tom Centolella, Carrie Chang, Elizabeth Chavez, Justin Chin, Eric Chow, Jorge Cortinas, Leslie Davis, Colette

DeDonato, Victor Diaz, Aja Duncan, Rebekah Eisenberg, Mahru Elahi, Ananda Esteva, Kathy Evans, Sauda Garrett, Russell Gonzaga, Toussaint Haki, Susanna Hall, Lenore Harris, Donna Ho, Le Hubbard, Uchechi Kalu, Carrie Kartman, Melissa Klein, Jaime Lujan, Margot Lynn, Michelle Matz, Scott Meltsner, Elizabeth Meyer, Doug S. Miller, Maiana Minahal, Peter Money, Dani Montgomery, Kim Nelson, Hoa Nguyen, Sharon O'Brien, Beto Palomar, Steve Parks, Andrew Pearson, Elissa Perry, Marcos Ramirez, Christina Ramos, Victoria Rosales, Yiskah Rosenfeld, Jime Salcedo-Malo, Johnna Schmidt, Margaret Schulze, Alison Seevak, Chris Sindt, giovanni singleton, Chad Sweeney, Luis Syquia, JoNelle Toriseva, Elsie Washington, Chris West, Marvin White, Canon Wing, Will Wylie, Gloria Yamato, and Tara Youngblood.

Thanks to WritersCorps Project Associate Avesa Rockwell who came through time and time again as an editor and administrator. Special thanks to Joan Pinkvoss and Gina Gemello and all the Aunt Lute staff for believing in the project and making it all work. Thanks to Adine Varah for her legal acumen and human heart. A final thanks to the San Francisco Arts Commission for its steadfast support over the past ten years and commitment to arts for all people.

City of One

contents

three OUR WORDS ARE UNIVERSAL

four PEACE IS HARMONY WITH THE THINGS AROUND YOU

five HOPE WAITS, LIKE US

six OURS POETICA

Introduction

Welcome to *City of One,* the WritersCorps anthology celebrating the 10th anniversary of our program. Since 1994, WritersCorps teachers—all accomplished writers—have taught creative writing to thousands of low-income youth. In public schools, youth detention centers, halfway houses, after-school programs, and many other community settings, young people have discovered the powerful process of writing. Sharing poems and stories about home, family, loss, and love, WritersCorps students have become an integral part of a growing community of writers.

In September 2003, WritersCorps was honored to receive the Espíritu Award for Peace and the Written Word from the Isabel Allende Foundation. With this opportunity, WritersCorps editor Colette DeDonato assembled a collection of writing by more than 150 diverse youth chronicling their responses to the ongoing violence permeating our culture—at home and around the world. American society is bombarded with political rhetoric and corporate solutions for peace, yet the voices of youth are dismissed, neglected, and even silenced. This book breaks that silence. *City of One* speaks to the profound and devastating impact of violence in young people's lives, and it is their passionate call for peace.

The book is also a world gathering: Haiti, Iran, China, Mexico, Yemen, Ukraine, and the United States are just a few of the countries represented in this diverse collection of writing. *City of One* faces head-on the hard questions about life in the inner city and in war-ravaged countries: Why must people suffer? Why is there so much violence? Why is there no peace? Whatever their race, ethnicity, or gender, whether they are eight or eighteen, living at home or far from home, these young writers express sadness, anger, and confusion—and yet, also great hope for survival in a difficult world. The youth in this book urgently tell us that the only way we can get to peace is to imagine it. Ultimately, the act of writing binds us together into a city of one.

WritersCorps is committed to providing opportunities for youth to write about their lives. As we've grown from an AmeriCorps pilot project to a national literacy model, we've worked to make writing an essential part of school, family, neighborhood, and community life. Our writers want to live in a world where all people are safe. For them, writing is a way of creating peace on the page and beyond. I am proud to share their work with you.

Janet Heller
Founder and Director
San Francisco WritersCorps
San Francisco, 2004

Foreword

One morning, in the spring of 2003, I found myself marching in the streets of San Francisco with my three grandchildren under a large PEACE banner which they'd painted. We were trying to stop the American government from invading Iraq. My youngest granddaughter was sitting on her father's shoulders, while the other two kids were holding my hands. We walked in a crowd of activists, old hippies, parents with babies, veterans in wheelchairs, and thousands of young people sharing a feeling of hope. I cannot forget all those young faces. Those kids had never experienced Vietnam or other similar conflagrations, yet they seemed as concerned about war as the older folks.

I have been in many protests and I have marched for peace innumerable times, to almost no avail. I have seen much violence in my life. I was born in the middle of the second World War, during the Holocaust, just before the atomic bombs hit Hiroshima and Nagasaki. I have seen military occupation, revolutions, and civil wars. I had to leave my country, Chile, after a brutal military coup in 1973, and I lived in exile with my family for thirteen years. I have good reason to wish for peace, but during that march in San Francisco I wondered why peace is so important to young Americans whose lives have been different from mine.

So I started asking. A nine year old told me that peace would be not being bullied. Someone added that peace begins when you hear what another person has to say. One girl informed me that in war more civilians die than soldiers, and many more women and children die than men. She told me that young people have everything to lose in an armed conflict, while the old men who start wars when it suits their interest are never at the front. She was clear about peace too: I have problems with my boyfriend but we don't hit each other, like my mom and my stepfather do. People can disagree but that doesn't mean that they should kill each other. Maybe these kids have not seen war firsthand, but certainly they have experienced violence in their short lives and know that they don't want it.

Several years ago I created the Isabel Allende Foundation, dedicated to supporting organizations that work for destitute women and children who need shelter, education, and better health. In 2003, a year marked by violence, the Foundation decided that its awards would focus on peace, because women and children cannot be protected without peace. As those kids told me in the march, peace starts in the family and in the community. Most of the Foundation's grant recipients work at a grassroots level. WritersCorps is one of these programs.

WritersCorps' goal is to give kids—many of whose lives are touched by poverty and violence—opportunities to develop their vision and voice through writing. As they write about their observations and feelings, these young people inevitably improve their learning skills and self-sufficiency.

2004 marks WritersCorps' ten-year anniversary. With terrorism and war in the air, they've chosen to celebrate the program's success by creating an anthology that shares ten years of youth writing on the subject of peace. *City of One* is that book.

I am moved when reading what these young people have to say about violence and peace in their lives; I am comforted by how much they care about the world. Today millions of human beings are massacred in ongoing wars and many more suffer the violence of poverty, yet our children believe that peace is possible. I share that belief. Although we have the awesome power to exterminate ourselves and to blow up the planet, I trust that we will do neither. Our destiny is not to perish, but to survive, progress, and evolve. And peace is the key. As a child said to me, peace begins in the heart of each one of us. We should listen to what our children are saying.

Many of the writers in this collection have had difficult lives. They come from many different backgrounds, and yet they all have in common grief and hope. They talk about finding redemption in the midst of violence. They write about drugs, guilt, loneliness, and about being lost. They long for love, friendship, loyalty, honor. A middle-school boy asks "Whose father did you kill in the war?" A young woman says that she lives in a world of worry. Another young man dreams of a home where he can shower alone, where the cops will not break in to take away his brothers, where he will wake up and his mother will be cooking in the kitchen. The basic joys of childhood are denied him, but he has the courage to write about them, as do others who write about family and urban life.

In spite of all the sadness and the anger experienced by these young writers, there is hope and light in these pages. The written word has a miraculous healing power; it cleans the wounds, eases the pain, leaves proud scars. The written word sorts out the confusion of life, gives us a voice, makes us strong, and connects us to other human beings. And when we are connected we are invincible! That is why I celebrate this extraordinary book written by young people who believe, as I do, that peace is not only possible, it is unavoidable. In order to make it happen, we have to imagine it and we have to describe it. The first step for making real the dream of luminous peace is to share it.

Isabel Allende
San Rafael, 2004

one

IN THE WORRY OF THE WORLD

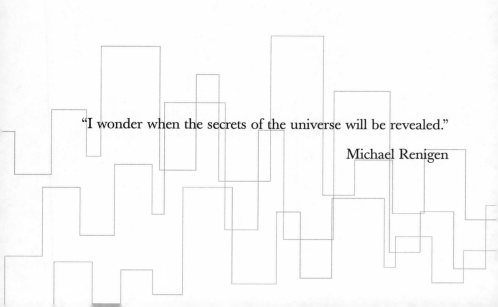

"I wonder when the secrets of the universe will be revealed."

Michael Renigen

Sitting by the Window
at Grandma's House

Sitting by the window at grandma's house.
The noon sun high up in the sky.
Too hot to go outside they say. Everything is closed.
The markets and shops that were opened early in the morning
were closed just minutes ago.
Sleep they say. But I can't sleep.
Grandma and grandpa are asleep.
Grandpa on his bed by the window,
the same one he sleeps on for years.
Grandma on her swinging bed called the *jula*.
It squeaks quietly while she sleeps.
Mother and everyone else are away
but it doesn't bother me that I am here alone.
Sitting by the window nothing bothers me.
I'm in this new world, away from my old self.
Away from the fast life of America. Here nothing bothers me.

I wake up from my thoughts when I hear the *azan*,
the sound of nearby mosques calling all to prayer.
I see men walking towards mosques, women
putting scarves on their heads while going into their houses to pray.
Some shops are closing, their owners hurrying to the nearest mosque.
Little boys run down their roofs where they were flying kites and run
to the mosque, stopping only to put their shoes on properly.

It is so peaceful seeing this little town.
Days go by slowly here, no need to rush,
everyone taking their time.
Muslims and Hindus living near each other
like two baby lambs sitting next to each other for warmth.
How can two religions coexist and not mind the differences
between beliefs and practices? But it is not always like this.
A few towns away the news of a temple being built over a torn
mosque causes trains with Hindus in them to be burned down.
The news of violence spreads, causing hatred like wildfire.
Muslim houses are being burned with the owners inside them.
Men, women and kids are being killed.
What once were two friendly neighbors are now enemies,
accusing each other.
There is no more trust or kindness.
Violence is being solved with more violence.
The wildfire grows all over India. Shops being burned,
people left homeless as if there weren't enough already.
The wildfire of hatred spreads and whatever it touches,
it destroys, like people's hearts.

Why can't people with different beliefs live together in peace?
Can't they ever accept each other? What needs to happen?
Will they ever look inside their hearts and learn to forgive?
Fighting is not worth it. As the wildfire moves faster,
it stops in the backyard of a poor house where two little boys,
one Hindu one Muslim, squat down on the dirt floor
to play marbles together, laughing secretly
because they know their parents will not allow this,
forgetting for a moment the rest of the country,
their parents yelling with hatred toward one another.

Can these two boys be their country's future
and stay innocent and open hearted?
Or will they grow up into adults and forget
what their hearts know is right?
In the distance, I hear my grandma calling me to pray.
I hurry up and put my scarf on and go,
praying for the peace of this sweet town.

Asefa Subedar, 19

Questions of the Universe

I wonder why
the world is
the way
it is.

I wonder why
people live
and they die.

I wonder when
the secrets
of the universe
will be
revealed.

Michael Renigen, 12

What Is

What is your anti-drug?
Who guards your soul?
What is your temptation?
Who crawls under your skin?
What is your limit?
Who do you stare at?
What made you?
Who do you love in the pit of your heart?
What enrages you?
Who do you bow to?
What crawled in you and died?
Whose father did you kill in the war?
What is everything?
Who is the great spirit?

Oscar Mangandid, 13

When Will It End

You may say they deserve it,
but do they really?
When will it end?
They bomb us,
we bomb them,
that's no help to the world peace we are trying to reach.

Their dying doesn't make those who died come back.
It is all about revenge.
We want them to feel the pain we feel,
the grief we feel,
the anger we feel.
But does that take us closer to world peace?
No.

Suzy Chen, 13

White Balloon

A white balloon
falls from the sky,
I stand, entranced,
wondering why.

A car's wheels roar past,
surely these moments
will be the balloon's last.

Yet...it bounces into
the safety of the gutter,
sure to be forgotten,
it lies among the muddy water
and the wet leaves so rotten.

Is it really better where it lies?

Is it better to avoid death only to suffer in life?

Or is it better to bite our lips and head through the strife?

Elina Ansary, 12

What Have You Done?

What have you done?
What makes you cry?
Who are you?
Who gives you joy and happiness?
Where were you?
What is your favorite number?
Where do you like to go?
Where would you fly to?
How many friends do you have?
Who do you talk to?
Where were you born?
What is your name?

Who's your boss?
What do you feel like?
What do you like to do?
Who do you want to be?
Are you happy?
When's your birthday?
What do you fear?
Who do you hate?
Where do you live?
Who makes you laugh?
How old are you?
What's your favorite subject and holiday?
Where did you come from?
What makes you speak?

Diana Marenco, 10

Dear Mr. Bush

Dear Mr. Bush why is public housing called projects,
Are we an experiment?

Dear Mr. Bush why do you shut down schools, lay off teachers
Yet build more prisons?

Dear Mr. Bush why do you throw all this dope in our
Poor communities and expect us not to touch it
Or do you?

Dear Mr. Bush why is it that when you became president
All this war started?

Dear Mr. Bush are you saying that it's OK to go to war?

Dear Mr. Bush why can you go to war and not go
To prison yet we get 25 to life for killing each other
On the streets?

      Ben I., 17

Compassion

Compassion
where have you been?
I done cussed out staff
been threatened with a pen

arguing relentlessly
cain't shut up
when I fall down
they make sure
I cain't get up

showing no remorse
hurting people's feelings
if anger was length
I'd be tall as the ceiling

they say love
is everlasting
where have you been?
I'm looking for compassion

Richard T. (a.k.a. Reno V.), 18

In the Mind

My fears are kept
in boxes in the basement,
and no one can know about them
except me.
My feelings are kept in the attic,
locked up,
so no one can hurt them or know about them.
Some windows are clean and some dirty,
so my mind can see what it wants to see.

There is a long stairway that never
ends, and not even I
can understand.

There is only one clock,
the Clock of Life,
and I don't know when it will stop.

In my mind there are solid doors
that look like a big maze
going on forever.
I don't have a key to all the doors.
I wonder when I will have the key
and can open them all up.

Yvette Martinez, 13

The Jungle

The jungle is a quiet place,
but little do you know,
it has many things waiting for you to see.

It has weird people,
strange animals
waiting for you for dinner,
weird jungle men and
undiscovered things
all living in harmony,
unlike us.

Jordan Declouette, 10

I Am in the World of Worry

I am in the world of worry
I have to worry about where I came from
I have to worry about who I am
I have to worry about my accent
I am in the world of worry
I have to worry about if I am fat or thin
I have to worry about what I have to eat
I have to worry about if my family or friends love me
I have to worry about who I should be friends with
I have to worry about who I should please
I have to worry about my skin color
I have to worry about what clothes and shoes I should wear
I have to worry about if I am safe
I am in the world of worry

Charlene Weah-Weah, 19

My 1st Birthday

I was born a young black man in 1982.
Right now it's 1983, my first birthday.
I can barely blow out my candles.
My cake is so big and the candles are so small.
I'm thinking of a way to blow out the candles
so I run outside to get the water hose
then run back in the house with the water hose.
Then my mother says, "Boy, what are you doing?"
My wish is too big for this small cake, Momma,
My wish is to give you eternal life.

Eric, 17

Frustrations

This is the year
we started a war.

This is the year
many innocent people will die,
young kids that don't have anything
to do with the war
will die.

This is the year we should
reunite
and make our lives better
and everyone's dreams come true.

This is the year we should
all live in peace,
then all my problems and frustrations
will go away.

Julissa Abigail Juarez, 14

Speaking Underground

When I dance
the legs of my Grandmother
lead me.
I dance to the Latin beat
she never heard
but was the lifeforce of
her grandparents.
I move my hands
her hands with their
long bony fingers with
tiny crescent moons at
each tip guiding
her way always.
When I speak
I speak with the voice
of my Grandfather.
I speak underground
in Spanish, in Russian.
Sometimes I use no
words at all.
I yell at a level they
were not allowed to use.
When I cry, I cry in
quiet and let the
warm tears flow
from my eyes like
their salty tears flowed
in silence.

My childhood was one
with flashy colors
and beautiful light.
I am growing up in a city.
I continue a journey
far from its
beginning.

The land
the perspective
the space
has all changed
and will change
more and more.

Our journey passes
through me,
the vessel which I am,
and I will carry it
and it will pass
out of me.

Gabby Cole, 17

What Do You Know
about African People

I walk down the street and a woman senses my accent
she asks
Do Africans live in trees?
And I go home and turn on the TV
see naked African children
begging for food
I walk to school and people make fun
of my accent
they ask me
Why do you talk like you have something in your throat?
I go to an African-American neighborhood
where I think I belong
Someone says
Why do you hate us?
And I say
the media makes you believe that we hate you
but we love you because we are the same people
we have the same blood
even though we don't speak the same language
then they ask
Why did you Africans sell us for money?
I tell them I can't speak for the past
They should ask the people who sold them
and the people who bought them

A little girl asks me if I speak Tarzan language
I go to the restaurant and someone asks me if we eat leaves
I go to the mall and someone asks me if we wear clothes
I go for a job interview and the boss asks me
if I left my home to labor for money in America
I fill out my application and someone asks
If I am from Nigeria or South Africa
maybe they don't know I'm from Liberia

Well, do you know that
oil and diamonds came from Africa?
Do you know that math was invented in Africa?
Do you know that education and writing began in Africa?
Do you know that beauty was started in Africa?
the kinky hair
you can do everything with it
you can braid it
you can straighten it
you can leave it like curly curly
Our eyes look peaceful
Like a flowing river
the full lips
big butt
people on TV want to look like this

Do you know that love, peace and forgiveness
came from Africa?

Because after all the slavery
loss of our homes
our families
after lynching us for being black
after working in the cotton fields
after breastfeeding white families' children
after working for free after beatings
after we watched our mothers
our sisters
our children being raped
after losing our land
our riches and our diamonds
after the bombing of our land
after taking our animals from Africa and putting them in the zoo
after destroying our self-esteem
after the media shows our bad side
I still forgive but I don't forget
And I know that love, peace, and forgiveness came from Africa

Tell me
What do you know about African?

Charlene Weah-Weah, 19

Ode to Sunset

First of amber, melt the sky,
what was blue has now turned pink.
Shore, the pink with the sea below,
silk so smooth it makes you cry,
reflects the light that's sent below.
Darts of heat pierce my skin,
reach the cave that I call heart.
See that no one lives in there,
ignite a flame of wild red,
first of ruby, melt the pain.

Rosa Alvarado, 12

Spirit

My spirit is a soul that lives in my life.
The breath I take is another life
toward the unfound spirit.
My spirit will love as long as I believe,
it is a force of love or hate.
My spirit-soul feels for nobody
but yet has enough love to last.
   My spirit lives in my mother
   and my mother's mother.
Death can't break it
but just make it stronger.
   My spirit breaks and dies only
   when I don't believe.

Kareem S., 17

Name Poem

Real story
a student is me
I come to America to have a good life
here there are too many special things to me
email me if you can do it
love is the best because it's funny, so funny...
a girl
she stands outside and sees
no matter
where you are
unforgettable
was when we were in love
that sky
that sea...

Rachel Fan Wu, 17

Journey of Emotions

Anger is the ocean wave, violently
hitting the shores.

Happiness is a mother
with her first child
she's ever had in her lifetime.

Sadness is losing someone you
deeply love, but don't want to express
your feelings.
Sadness is Cookie Monster
without his cookie.

Love is when you can't talk
your mind goes blank and your heart stops.
Love is white.
It can be silent or loud.

Anxiety is not knowing
if something is really wrong
until it happens.

Peace is all different people getting
along and being happy.
Peace is love for one another
even though you are totally
different from each other.

Hope
is feeling so lonely that you
will accept anything that comes along
even if she is not the right person.
Hope is a baby bird waiting
to learn how to fly
out of its
overcrowded
nest.

Fear is the rainforest
losing its trees, animals and all hope.

Safety is a neighborhood
with no guns
or people drunk
on the street.

Freedom is a golden
eagle flying across the grassy
hilltops
of Arizona.

Cierra Crowell, 10

Baby Bits

When those babies get blown to bits,
I laugh with my friends.

Then those child workers collapse from exhaustion,
and I begin my algebra homework.

When people fear for their lives
and I feel hungry.

Oh yes, this injustice is horrible,
and so is that hairdo,
time to go to the mall.

I hate unfairness and exploding pigs,
What will I wear tomorrow?

How could those executives care only about money?
Please give me some bucks for a CD player.

Sorry to say, but I'm fine here,
I'm happy,
I'll be safe and lucky,
without even trying,
well, I'll just hope that those worlds don't collide.

Grace Harpster, 13

Macau

America is a mountain and I can't climb.
America is a killer in my home.

Macau is a dictionary and I am a word,
a battery and I am a clock,
rain water and I am a field thirsty for rain.

Ryan Tang, 17

Some Day

In the perfect world
there will be no nuclear bombs,
no wars, no drugs, and no gangs.
There will be more medicines
for bad illnesses
and all people will respect each other
regardless of race, nationality or language.

In the perfect world
there will be peace and love.

Juan Angel Sarmiento, 15

Going to God's Place

For me to get here
it took nine long hard months

When I leave here
I am going to God's Place

I am going to take
history with me

For me to get here it took
time and patience

When I leave here
I am going to another planet

I am going to take technology and peace

For me to get here
it took different races

When I leave here
I am going to take my jokes
and personality

For me to get here
it took being committed

When I leave
I am bringing my knowledge

I am going to take a dictionary

Tatiana Stewart, 15

Nico

I am Dominiq Wright
quick, funny, and smart

Nico who can be ready to fight
like a bulldog
but nice inside

who believes people can speak their mind

who thinks we should have peace in the world
who wants the world to stop these wars

who can be slick like a snake
and shy at the same time

who hopes we will all
have afterlives

who imagines all people
with real homes and real food

who wonders what New York
would be like if those planes didn't crash

I am Nico
who shows respect in the best way
who shows his feelings through writing
and lives his life
and explores his life
the way he wants

who can be quick like a cat
staying on my own two feet

Dominiq Wright, 13

What Is a River?

A river is life,
everybody needs water.

It is history,
opening antiquity's secret.

The river is a yellow silk braid
warming the earth.

Apple Li, 17

Haiku

Sun and moon,
bright and dark,
again and again every day.

Joseph Beck, 11

two

UNDER FIRE

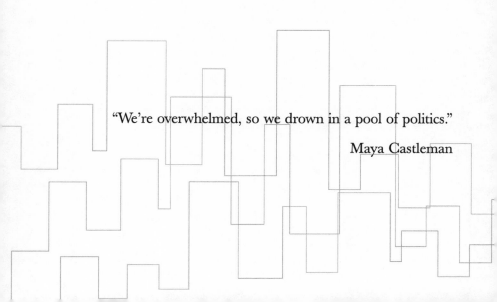

"We're overwhelmed, so we drown in a pool of politics."

Maya Castleman

On the Road to Inner Peace

We survive war and conquest; we survive colonization, acculturation, assimilation; we survive beating, rape, starvation, mutilation, sterilization, abandonment, neglect, death of our children, our loved ones, destruction of our land, our homes, our past, and our future. We survive, and we do more than just survive. We bond, we care, we fight, we teach, we nurse, we bear, we feed, we earn, we laugh, we love, we hang in there, no matter what.

—Paula Gunn Allen

Just imagine, if we all felt a sense of peace within ourselves, then we'd communicate and work with each other better, which would lead to healthier communities struggling together towards social change and justice. It is our responsibility to search and find within ourselves that inner love, which can lead to a sense of inner peace. The internal, personal struggle I am facing in my spiritual faith and daily life often becomes overwhelming. I've internalized the racism and sexism that this white, patriarchal, capitalist system has used against us to destroy our communities and to chip away at our self-worth. It's easy to fall into a depressive state of self-pity and hopelessness, because often times, we are made to feel powerless. The feeling of isolation can make us feel as if we are all alone in our struggles. In a sense we have been conquered and divided against each other. An Afrikan proverb rings true, "when there are no enemies within, there are no enemies outside."

With all the crimes committed against humanity, from the environmental racism in poor, people-of-color communities such as Hunter's Point in San Francisco to the unsolved serial murders and disappearances of women in Cuidad Juarez, there can be no peace without justice. And there can only be peace if all people are given an equal chance to live, breathe clean air, drink clean water, eat healthy food, and practice what they believe to be a peaceful path. Like the Zapatistas, we must be able to govern ourselves, to make our own laws, and unite our people into strong communities.

It is through prayer and ceremony that I find the strength within to clarify my role and purpose. I am reflecting on how I can impact my family and community the most. We can make huge impacts with the simplest of actions, such as tutoring our younger brothers and sisters, or serving ice cream on hot sunny days. It doesn't matter how much money someone makes. It is the daily efforts that every person makes—from the janitors to the farm workers—that lead to social change. Like the way a fire spreads, the way it begins with a spark that lights into a flame and bursts into a fire, that's how change and peace will spread. I know that sometimes life's demands can become so overwhelming that you think you can't make a change. To me it doesn't matter how many peace/anti-war rallies you attend. What matters is the consistent love you demonstrate in your everyday life in your community.

It is important to find your own path and find the things to inspire you to get up, speak up, write up, draw up, make up, think up. The fact that something you dream of has never been done before should not stop you in seeking a new path. This isn't an easy task, it requires a lot of energy, time and effort. You have all the answers within you. All the love you need is with and around you.

I once read, "What we can easily see is only a small percentage of what is possible. Imagination is having the vision to see what is just below the surface; to picture that which is essential, but invisible to the eye." I try to keep this in mind on those days when nothing makes sense. It helps me to find clarity through love by healing, heal through love, and see with clarity to find peace within.

Deborah Gallegos, 23

Incognito

I think 90% of me is Darkness.
The other 10% of me is good,
    pure, and clear as crystal.
I have lived in seclusion for so long, I can't relate
to people long enough to love them.
So I keep my distance.
I cannot predict the future, only live in the present
and watch the clock tick and stay tucked in the Dark.

    Cleavon, 17

OUTside/INside

I am always on the inside
    of some dysfunctional situation
Trying to get out.
Since I'm different I'm always in someone's gossip
Who doesn't know what I am about.
I stay on the inside
    of my poems and books and poetry.
I am always searching
    to find love and essence inside of me.
I am always in the middle of a good conversation
When someone cuts me off,
But hardly ever between cover and blankets
    that feel soft.
I enjoy being inside my writing zone
Though I dread always being inside, being alone.

I am always on the outside of some stupid inside joke
And I don't mind always being outside the doors
    of people who smoke.

I am always on the outside
    because that's where I love to be
Because it makes me feel free.
When I least expect it I find myself outside
    of yet another circle of friends,
And I'll go inside to rest
    when the failing of our people ends.
Outside in the earth I find myself once more,
Outside of oppression I am seeking
    all that life has in store.
Looking around out here
I see that people on the inside have been
Won over by fear.
I wish I wasn't always outside of the house for love,
But I do search inside to find guidance from above.
I belong on the outside of sistas who don't care
And of young people quickly going nowhere.
But people try to pull me into the realm of the night
And of those who refuse to try and do right.

Natriece Spicer, 18

Twelve Days

12 winos drinking
11 crackheads tweaking
10 rats eating
9 hookers hookin'
8 dogs barking
7 babies crying
6 cats sleeping
5 robbers creeping
4 gangs shooting
3 guys screaming
2 cars rocking
and a hobo taking a pee.

Cameron Contos-Slaten, 12

Never Safe

I am never safe,
never safe in a world of hate.
Gangsters, haters,
just plain scary people following me down
the street.
But you'll protect me,
won't you?

Terrorists, bombers, kidnappers,
scarin' me to death
with scary tales told by my friends.
Never safe in a world of hate.
But you'll protect me,
won't you?

When you're here I feel safe,
not carin' about the hate
because I know you'll protect me.

Grace Sizelove, 12

Under Fire

Back in the day
there weren't so many problems,
no war, no guns.

Now we destroy:
It's all we do,
all we're good at.

Back in the day
there were no bombs, no explosions,
only simple talk of finding a home.

Now we have homes,
and we fight over them
instead of sharing.

Back in the day
life was better
than these days under fire.

Marco Moon, 15

We Drown

Take down the posters,
rip up the ads,
stop the word of mouth.

There's no more involvement,
we cry,
but we sit,
we're overwhelmed,
so we drown in
    a pool of politics.

        Maya Castleman, 12

Far Away

I see people destroying the forest.
I feel like crying because many birds
will not have homes.

I see the mountains
destroyed,
many people sharing one house,
so small,
and a little child
trying to make his kite fly higher.

The buildings are ugly and poor.
No one has a mirror to see themselves.
The people are so poor
they are eating from the trash,
and taking a bath in the wide streets.

I see a mother and a child
sleeping on the sidewalk,
an entire family riding on one motorcycle,
very dangerous.

I see Jerusalem,
many people praying to God,
and in Germany many killed
for no reason.

I've seen many bad things today,
things I've never seen before.

Dexter (Jerwin) Dizon, 13

In the Real World

I think right now
cars are being blown up by bombs,
gangs are fighting on the streets,
kids are fighting kids,
adults are fighting adults.
I think right now
there is murder,
and the family members are crying,
poor people are starving without food,
people are working hard to get money.
I think right now people are trying to survive.

Armando Mejia, 12

Fog and Peace

I am from wars in far
off lands,
blistering sun and slavery,
no peace of mind
or physical at all.

There is fog cover thick as
we smile, blankly.

Oppressors try to flood us
with their thoughts,
their ways,
try to hold down my religion.

They can try to fan away
the smell of sizzling potatoes
cooking in grease, but don't succeed.

Shalom is what my people
stand for peace, Shalom
we live, strive and are
forever reaching since Moses
and our way of life
revolves around it.

Israel strives and I just
sit watching the fog and
cry.

Maya Castleman, 12

War

The weapon is walking to the enemies.
The gun spits out a bullet to the people.
The bomb is flying to the house with the red mailbox.
The missile is flying to the tall building where people work.

The weapon is walking to the enemies.
The sword is going into a boy's belly.
He cries and shouts at the sword.
The tank is going to the farms to trample grains down.

The weapon is walking to the enemies.
The gun is crying when he spits out a bullet
at the people who scream.
The bomb has a pang of sorrow when he flies to the house
where the baby is sleeping.
The sword is crying when he goes into the boy's belly
because the sword doesn't want to remove
one boy's life and dreams.

The weapon is walking to the enemies
while they are crying and sad.
They feel very sorry and don't want to fight
with other countries.
Their host's eyes have blood and swords and fury.

Bora Kim, 16

The Mystery of Cheetahs

No one knows what a cheetah is.
All we know is that cheetahs are swift,
brilliant, graceful, pretty, and cunning.

Cheetahs move through the jungle
with poise and attitude
until,
one day,
out of nowhere.

BANG!

Cheetah handbag.

Don't laugh.
It isn't funny.

Elizabeth Thompson, 12

Home

Home is a telephone
half a blunt and
toilet bowl

Home is havin' ma brothers and sisters wake me up
in the mornin' to tell me moma's cookin

Home is that warm air that bites you
when you first walk through the door

Home is showerin' by yo self

Home is a place where there ain't no police
in the neighborhood telling me I cain't
enjoy being outside wit ma people

Home is any place but an institution

My home is filled wit crack rocks and dope spots

My home is constantly invaded
by crooked cops whose purpose is to send
my people to jail instead of helpin' them

My home has no strong black men
My home is filled with women that try
very hard but can't
teach a boy to be a man

My home is filled with racism

My home is filled with youth that have
no dreams of being successful
by going to school

My home is broken

Greg E. (a.k.a. Pistola), 18

Black vs. Latino Fight at ISA

slap face fight break race
school rage kid lead chase
find truth close friend gone
think win shrug lose face

International Studies Academy Group T'ang Poem

T'ang is a style of classical Chinese poetry from the T'ang Dynasty.

Regret

Keep doing what
I do, I find
myself in a ditch.
Electric chairs,
ropes around my body,
clinched.

I want to live
life full of respect.
Things I done did
I will always
regret.

Everick S., 18

Safety Issues

Wanting to shut my TV off,
throwing my radio across the room.
It sounds like the blast of the Twin Towers,
a thousand times softer.
Trying to calm the voices in my head.
It's aching when you can't find 5,000 dead.
They say they want stretchers.
For what? Body parts and heads?
Races, colors, faces, dreams, unbelievable.
The images coming through my TV screen
of one after the other
Twin Towers falling to the streets.
Turned off my TV, wanting to get away.
It's all I can read: newspaper after newspaper,
article after article, picture after picture.
Things are going cold in me.
Don't stop our normal lives, they say.
But we can't get regular programmin' on MTV.
They say, *Go back to work,*
nothing to worry about.
I think everyone is standing still,
waiting for a pin to drop,

or the next plane to crash, the next bomb to go off.
Such a fast-paced world, never stopping.
Nothing's normal, never has been.
Now we're just not moving at all.

Safety. Safety has never changed for me.
My security, my government, senators, congress
are my family, loved ones, close friends—
the love I have for another
and the love they show me.
Forget the President, PoPos, or the IRS.
They don't know me.
Never done anything for me but bombed other places,
slammed people's faces into car doors,
handcuffed innocent people, and
taken down drug lords for the millions of cash that they got.
Seeing crying faces, hearing sirens, revving engines,
frantic people running.
I run to my family, my mother and father,
and feel safe.

Cynthia A., 17

What I've Seen

I need to write about
all the hatred in this world,
all the racist people,
all the wars, the fights, the arguments.
I've seen too many people in pain,
like a bird without its nest
trying to find a home.
I've seen little girls
cry in their moms' arms,
making it harder for their mothers
to go on
because they don't want
to see their daughters in pain—
to see them crying.
I've seen it,
and I know how it is,
because I was one
of those little girls.

Zelkja Lazic, 15

The Projects

The projects are filled with drugs and thugs,
feels like being stuck in a black box
with an angry green fox, and guns hot
after a shot.

A stripped car feels naked with no tires,
the ground dirty with diapers and blood,
stained from a fight two months ago.
A drunk man shatters a bottle of 211,
and money is sad because you don't have a job,
standing on the corner selling rocks.

The air is wheezing from all the weed smoke.
After a dogfight, the cold, dead
body of a dog lying with no soul.

The building's body aches
from the loud music
and people staying out all night.

Tazia Payne, 13

Ghetto State of Mind

The life I live is violent
killers, hustlers, playas, and innocent bystanders all in one.
But this is how I chose to live.
Sitting on my block getting money,
being a negative role model for little kids.
Why did I choose to live the way I lived?
Is it because I wanted to thug all my life,
and supply rocks for dope fiends' pipes?
Or is it because I'm trapped in a cage full of rage,
ready to flip the page and go into that savage phase?
I can't call it.

Young cats killing each other over drugs and turfs,
trying to see a meal ticket.
I know my family doesn't want to pick out my casket,
living this life they'll be forced to pick it.
Sometimes when I'm asleep at night I have dreams
of my life coming to an end.
You might call these nightmares, to me these are dreams.
Maybe because it comes with the package,
this life is all hood, caskets are all wood,
this life is too much for me.
Too much killing, too much crime.

Too many young brothas killing their own people
for the price of a dime.
Too many sisters not knowing who they baby daddy is,
because they didn't trip off who they was with
before they handled they biz.
Too many little kids growing up without their fathers;
because they so-called father ran out
because he couldn't handle his responsibility.

But technically that's the way the game goes
when you living this ghetto life,
with struggling and strife,
where you got to fight to win your rights.
'Cause in this life ain't nothing free.
The poor stay poor,
the rich get more chips,
and dope dealers live ghetto fabulous
with all the baddest chicks.

But now, me personally, I'm through with this life of crime.
But can't nobody change my ghetto state of mind.

Charles K., 19

Red and Death

Yesterday I was red.
Death is red. Violence
is gangs. Trouble is gangs.
Drugs are worse than eating
a big bug. Drugs cause death.
If I die I pray that I will
go to heaven. Kill is what
gangs do with guns and knives.
The world is dangerous
because of gangs. Someday
I will be dead because
of gangs. I would rather sleep
and kiss my mother.

Cynthia Lopez, 12

The Ghetto Curse

U say u want to be a thug
on the corner, slangin' drugs.
Was it a lack of luv?
Now u want to fill a brother with slugs.
Just because u packin' a gat
doesn't mean u got it like that.
Live by the gun u die by the gun,
that is a fact.
Gettin' yo head pumped up off a rap,
then u go out there and get smoked like a joint.
Now let me get to the point.
If you continue the ghetto curse
u might just end up in a hearse.

Dartanian K., 18

Hope

Gangs use drugs.
Gangs hope on violence
to take their anger out,
help them forget about
abusive parents,
poverty.
I guess they can't dream
of their parents' love.
Maybe if they ask their parents
at home, tears in their eyes.

Jimmy Phetthiraj, 12

Gangster

I am a young student living in the ghetto.

I see people fighting in the street
about who are better gangs.
I see people doing drugs on the street corner
trying to hide on the side of a car.
I see people shooting in the street
about their color.

I am a young, scared student.

As I walk toward the 19 Polk bus stop,
I see people staring at me real bad
'cause of my race.
I see people following me
and asking me for a dollar.

I am a young, scared student.

Living in a ghetto
is not that easy.

Philip Bautista, 14

Never Safe

Murder,
seeing people in body bags,
hearing about the latest gang fight
or rape,
finding needles or a bullet
on the ground,
knowing you're never safe,
feeling you have nowhere
to belong,
being an outsider,
never staying in one place
really long.
Hearing about the world
and its problems.
Running the race
never to win.

Knowing that people aren't even
your friends.
Every so often you hear someone yell,
or maybe you see someone being
violated,
manipulated,
underestimated,
and still you don't stop
and help.
The first thing we think is
he deserved it or maybe
he is just playing.
But it's not all that funny
when it's you or me.

Jermaine LeBrane, 13

My Story

I have a brother that I love very much,
but he treats me badly
as if he hates me
and my mom doesn't do anything about it.
He says that I don't learn anything in school,
he calls me a *bura*, then my mom
says she is going to take me out of school.

But I want to stay in school.
That's why I work at McDonald's six days
every week and six hours every day.
It's very difficult for me because
I leave work at 12:00 midnight
and when I get home I have to do
my studies. I go to sleep very late
and wake up at six in the morning
to come to school.
Sometimes I'm very tired at school
and fall asleep during class.
Sometimes I don't have the energy
to continue, but I think to myself
that if I don't study I won't advance my life.

I don't recommend this to anyone,
to work and go to school.
It's very difficult.

Yesis Lazo, 16

Dreams

If dreams die,
life is like
a country with no citizens,
a school with no teachers,
a kite with no line,
a sky with no sun,
a fishpond with no liquid.

Michael Xiao, 17

three

OUR WORDS ARE UNIVERSAL

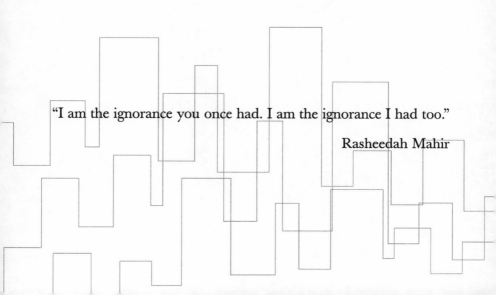

"I am the ignorance you once had. I am the ignorance I had too."

Rasheedah Mahir

Paz Comienza Contigo
(Peace Starts with You)

I remember the words my Great-Grandmother once said. "Paz comienza contigo, paz comienza con vosotros." Peace starts with you, peace starts with us. I wondered what those words meant. Words that came out of her mouth like an ice-cold margarita on a hot summer day. Words that came from her heart through her veins and out her mouth like baby birds wanting to reach the sky. Words that come straight from the bottom of my heart, and they reach you by the wind blowing outside my bedroom window. Words that travel through the warm satin streets smile beneath my window.

As I remember those words, I think about how we now live in a world torn by conflict. I think about what President Bush is doing in Iraq. President Bush is out of his mind, attacking a city with little children running barefoot, screaming as they see bombs coming down on them like rain. People do not understand that war does not make peace. Innocent people, who are doing nothing more than wanting to live their normal lives, are dying. What is war? It's not just between countries, it's between brothers and sisters, aunts and uncles, communities and gangs. How can we have peace between countries, when we don't even have peace in our own homes? Brothers and sisters are killing each other because of a misunderstanding.

Fear is also a big part of this. I think that many people fear peace because we are not used to having it. We are so used to living without peace, do we even know what peace looks like? Have you ever seen it? Heard or smelled it?

Armando Aguilar, 14

Waiting

I come from
a long line
of people who
divided the men
from the women.
I come from
a long line of darkness
and hate. I come from
a long line of people
who let their fear
take over. I come
from a long line
of no light.
I come from
a long line
of people where
you have to wait,
wait, and wait
to get what you want.
The line I am in
is the world
upside down.
I make a mistake,
and I start all over
again.

Robby Macam, 12

Mystical

Call me mystical water,
wiser than a warrior princess.
Call me gentle silence in the air.
I become the mystical wolf
wandering in my life.
I am the wolf protected
by the moon shield.

Stephanie Membreno, 12

In My City of One

I traveled on a boat to my city.

You see, I was a rich person and I loved my people. I kept no guard next to the door. One night, a robber came into my house and stole 200 dollars. I left my village because I did not trust my people anymore.

Then, when I got to my city, nobody was there. I said to myself, "Well, I will be safe here." Then I was all alone. I said to myself, "On the other hand, I don't have anybody to talk to."

I was so sad.

Amy Guadalupe Medina Villa, 9

I Am

I am the ghetto slums
drug sellin baby boy who
thought the squeaky closet
was a ghost
I was the weed smoke
lingering in my lungs
the excitement that
picked up the gun
I am the choice that took
my freedom from me
the rain that sprinkled on me
I am the dream
that will one day be
free

Lawrence W., 17

Do Not Call Me

inspired by Diane Burns' poem, "Sure You Can Ask Me a Personal Question"

How am I?
I do not know how I am
I am an Arab
I am not a terrorist
I am not a suicide bomber
I am Arab
I am Muslim
with a great faith
I am a guy with a great mind
I am Arab with the love of this country

Oh, so you like Osama Bin Laden?
    That close
Oh, so you have an Arab lover?
    That tight
Oh, so you have an Arab wife?
    Yes, with two children

I do not know how they get into this world
I am not a terrorist
I worry about the United States more than anyone
I like her people more than anyone
Yes, some of them call me Spanish
some of them call me Chinese
No, I am Arab from Yemen
and I say to the whole world
I am an Arab guy
I am Arab
I am Arab
I am Arab

Safwan Alzindani, 16

I Come From

I come from the sky.
I come from a window of fresh air.
I come from a place in my family.
I come from the center of the earth
    with God Jesus and love.
Where do you come from?
Do you know me?
Do I know you?
I come from a shoe, a book, do you?
I know me, do you?
I come from a world full of questions,
a world full of food.
I am the queen.
I am royalty.
You call me by my name.
I call you by yours.
You can call me Sharina Love.
You can call me Hope, Respect,
    or Black Mother Earth.
But call me by my name.

Sharina Weatherspoon, 11

Magic

With my hands I can feel
the air when I'm in a car.
With my magic hands I can feel
the majestic sky
breezing through my fingers.

With my eyes I can see
people rushing and walking downtown
living their lives.
With my magic eyes I can see
the bright, dazzling heavens
and God looking down on all His creation.

With my tongue I can taste
the most savory and delicious steak on earth.
With my magic tongue I can taste
the bitterness of revenge, cold as ice.

With my ears I can hear fire sirens
rushing
to a burning building.
With my magic ears I can hear the cries
of families with passed away loved ones.

With my nose I can smell the scent
of beautiful flowers in a flower shop.
With my magic nose I can smell the blood
of a fallen soldier
in a pointless war.

Emmanuel Caramat, 13

Baraka

They are dancing.
I think they are dancing for the rain.

Birds start to fly and then appears
a waterfall with a rainbow.

A lake reflects the sky,
then a sunrise on the water.

A falcon in a tree.
The trees are green mixed with yellow.
I think the people are cutting down the jungle
to make a city.

A sad man is watching
the people from the city
destroy the forest.

In Brazil the people are fixing
their houses, and looking
out the window. Buildings without paint,
clothes hanging from the windows
to dry.

We see how some people make cigarettes
with hard work,
then other people smoke the cigarettes easily.

I feel bad for all these people
that died in the war in Iraq.

And the baby chickens, how the people
throw them like they are nothing.

Marco A. Ramírez, 16

I Bit into Life

I bit into life and felt the spirit in me:
Tastes so beautiful, so sweet, so lovely.
I could have this on my plate any day,
Any hour, any moment.

I bit into life and I knew the color of the sky,
Felt so wonderful seeing birds and colored
butterflies.

I bit into life and my eyes flew open
I'm not blind anymore, so now I can see.
I know when people look back at me.

I bit into life and knew this was love
Before, I had no idea what I was made of.

I bit into life and took my first breath
Tasted great, felt so fresh.

Thea Matthews, 15

Inside of Me Are Many Rooms

In the house of my mind
my family is walking around
trying to get dinner ready.

In the house of my mind
there is a room
that is locked
trying to keep my anger from getting away.

In the house of my mind
there is an open room
filled with happiness and peace.

In the house of my mind there are many rooms
made of glass
that lets the sun shine inside
and makes the darkness go away.

I can go up into a room
and see the whole world.
I can see kids and people starving for food,
waiting for someone to help them.
I can see the twin towers fall.
I can see the white house becoming
a place of darkness and anger.
I can also see George Bush
trying to start a war with Iraq.

Luis Miguel Bravo, 13

Sending

I'm sending a check to my mom so she can go to a
better college.
I'm sending a peace flag to Iraq.

I'm sending food and food stamps to the poor.
I'm sending my mom and dad home from work to rest
because they work too much.

I'm sending education to the world,
and homes to the poor.

I'm sending strength to the disabled,
and responsibility to the youth.

I'm sending light to the night.
I'm sending my neighborhood art
because it needs to be colorful.

And I'm sending my neighborhood peace.

Peter Amaya, 12

Love Is Everywhere

Love is everywhere.
    Love is in the smile of the little baby
who is playing in a park.
    Love is in the beautiful rose
which burns in the morning
and adorns the garden.
    Love is in your mother
who wakes up early
to make a good breakfast
for her children.
    Love is a couple who always
are together in good things and bad,
always showing their love.
    Love is in a friend
who is always there for you, making
you feel happy.
    Love is a word with
a stronger meaning.
    Love is like a garden,
you enjoy it and you have to care for it,
so it will be a good and beautiful garden.
    Love is in yourself,
you only have to give it
and receive it.
    Love means peace, happiness
and smiles.
    Love is the power of all the world.

Antonia Soto Arias, 18

Seeds That Can't Grow

I'm sending my soul
to revive all the people who died
on September 11th.
I'm sending hope to everyone
that the war will stop.

I'm sending water to seeds
that can't grow.

I'm sending my neighborhood money
to pay the bills.

I'm sending the love of my life a rose
that will last a lifetime.

Raymond Saechao, 13

Friend Who

Friend who goes with me to the mosque
every Friday, who says funny things,
who is sad when he gets in trouble,
who helps me with my math homework,
who goes with me to the park every Saturday
and Sunday, who shares his lunch with me
if I forgot mine.

Bashir Algaheim, 14

Oath of Friendship

I will be your friend
until the earth loses its weight,

until my heart is broken,

until I can't breathe,

until the fish can fly
and the birds can swim,

until the moon becomes bigger
than the sun,

until the bridges are made
of rainbows.

          Guan Feng, 17

No Paper No Books

for the Rev. Martin Luther King Jr.

When I heard Black children's classrooms
had no chairs
no paper
no books
and no pens
I felt angry like you.
I am a person of color in America too.
I see things are not equal.

Before I came here,
I believed all people would be equal
in America
because your dream came true.
But we need to work hard
to keep the dream alive.

Jia Jian Lin, 17

We Are Sisters

I am the moon and my brother is the sun
I am the god who rules the world
I am the earth who's as wise as you
I am the calendar that has all the dates of the year
I am the light that shines
I am the wrinkled hands that my grandma has from working
I am the feather in the sky
I am the tree that falls to give you oxygen
I am the snow that's on top of the mountain
I am the watch that works
I am the cross around your neck
I am the angel behind your back

Mission Girls Group Poem

I Am

I am the first spoken word of Swahili
that flowed like the river into Africa
I am the river that formed the mother and father of the world
I am the confidant of the king
the princess
daughter of Safria
I am the beauty of my land
I am the first fruit put into the basket on Kwaanza
And there again the beautiful song of
the spoken language
I am Aunt Jemima binding the family
I am Harriet Tubman
Dr. Martin Luther King freeing my people
I am the Black Panther in the souls of the righteous leaders
I am the June in Juneteenth
the celebration of my soul
I am the wild in the animals of Africa
I am the first African to set foot
on the moon
I am the inventor of all inventors
I am the future of my culture

Stephanie Dunlap, 19

What Makes Me Myself

I come from math because every part of my body
is a fraction, a decimal, and a percentage.
My mathematics knowledge makes me myself.

The color blue is the color of the sky, the color of the ocean.
My favorite color is the color of myself.

Pizza—ah, pizza—is one of the foods that make me myself.
I have a lot of friends, like the toppings on a pizza.

Superman is my kind of superhero.
He can fly high, he can fly low, he can fly fast, he can fly slow.
He is as strong as an ox. I want to be Superman and fly,
or a karate master who punches and kicks really fast.

The violin's sound is a rhythm in my heart that heals my wounds.

I am safe in my bedroom because it is a really private place.
Mexico is the place I would rather be instead of San Francisco.

I am the yin and yang of the Chinese symbol.

Sweetheart is the one name you should not call me
or you will feel deep pain.

Speaking five languages makes me more sociable.

I love swimming in the summer, in the river, in the lake,
with the fish, being like the fish.
I am happy as a dog wagging my tail.

I am the moon in the night sky.
I am the sky where my friends,
the moon and the stars, hang from.

Orion Royce Macario, 11

See Me

I am the boxes of trash
waiting to be taken to the dump.
My emotions
are students laughing,
a book in the old attic.

My eye is a building being painted.

My body is made of flowers
stepped on, shoe marks all over me.
I am the church with singing
bells and trees surrounding me,
a mountain watching planes fly by,
a bird searching for food.

I am a plant seeing my reflection
in a puddle.

Rosy Mena, 13

My Face

My eyes are like a planet cut in half, showing the core.
My nose is a vacuum that sucks in air and pushes it out.
My cheeks are like cushions.
My eyebrows are strips of grass growing over my eyes.
My hair is like the tops of trees.
My teeth are big mashing machines.
My mouth is a wing flapping up and down.
My ears are like big valleys.
My eyelids are like shades.
My eyelashes are barriers catching things
that fall from above.

Seth Gossage, 10

Seeing Clearly

I am the stars,
the moon, and the queen of the earth.
I am the ground many folks walk on and litter.
I am the concrete,
spreading miles and miles,
connecting concrete walls.

I am the knife,
the gun,
and the drugs that killed you.
I am the metal structure of your overcrowded building.

I am the 7 cents an hour paid overseas,
the 10 cents an hour paid in my own city.
I am these means streets, every day.

I am the torture of my slave ancestors,
the ship that kidnapped them.
I am the weave and the braids,
the nappy thick hair,
takes hours to comb.

I am the thought
you think now.
I am the conversation you will have later on tonight.
I am the dream
you do remember.
I am the dream
Martin Luther King Jr. had.

I am the life,
soul, and spirit of a woman.
I am a woman who loves my women.
I am the ignorance you once had.
I am the ignorance I had too.
I am the child with no food to eat,
the child on drugs.

I am those signs held up in a demonstration.
I am the microphone,
loud strong voice.
I am the organizing,
the Power,
the Word.
I am the flyers posted all over town.
I am this revolution.
I am that political prisoner.
I am
I am
I am not blind,
not no more,
I am not blind.

Rasheedah Mahir, 18

The Peace

The peace I hear
is the sound of birds calling me for a fly up in the sky.
The peace is the silence I hear around me.
The peace I hear
is the whale calling me to see its action.
The peace I hear
is the wind blowing across my face.
The peace I hear
is the laughter at the table at Eid.
The peace I hear
is the turtle sitting in the sun shining brightly.
The peace I hear
is the grass moving here and there.
The peace I hear
is the dolphin jumping up and down in the water.
The peace I hear
is the tree's leaves shaking, singing the night sky.

Saman Minapara, 10

My Friend

I see you there.
I see you there in my kindergarten class.
I spill the juice and it is spreading all over.
I know the teacher is coming back
and then I see you there,
helping me.

I see you at recess.
Nobody that I can play with
and I feel so cold.
But you ask me to play
and I feel warm again.

Lily Nguyen, 10

four

PEACE IS HARMONY WITH THE THINGS AROUND YOU

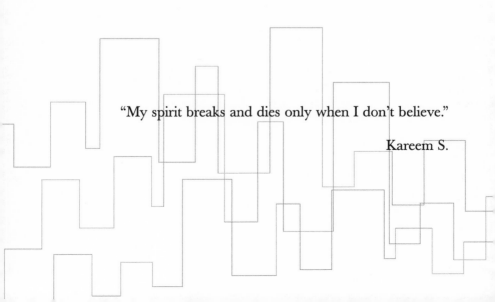

"My spirit breaks and dies only when I don't believe."

Kareem S.

My People

My people are the earth's handwriting,
earth's tattoos, earth's paintings, earth's wrinkles,
earth's cracks that have healed.

My people are a storm which opens its ruby eye
to a reflection of desert, mountains, humans and earth,
whose eyelashes beat the sky like an eagle's wing
and move its way through a blind night.

My people are a shapeless language
written in the milky clouds on early spring mornings
that taste like sweet red cherries.

My people are the dark scars of history.
My people are chapped lips and dry hands.
My people are giants
sleeping with hard, jagged blankets
over smooth bodies
who to us are heavenly mountains.

My people are a vanishing ocean
That's fading away slowly as if someone was smearing
its painting full of colors.

My people are in a red, brick and dirt pot
made with smooth, soft clay,
which inside holds water,
pure, clean mountain water
unlike the water which runs from their faucets.

My people are skies and oceans on fire,
the trees and rain giving birth to flowers
and are the grounds opening up to a new level
of potential.

My people are the seeds,
seeds that will one day
move the grounds beneath them.

My people are all people.
My people are you.
You are the storm,
you are the flowers,
you are the scars and the oceans
and the heavenly mountains.

You are the seeds that move the ground.

Sadaf Minapara, 15

Morning Glory

Soft leaves run
up and down the gate
leading to the
blue-violet blossom.

M'kia McCright, 13

Family Night Out

The moon is out
and the kids makin' funny noises with their mouth.
Aunts, uncles, nephews, nieces, mom and dad, brothers, sisters
are at Grampa's farm in a circle
in the cold keeping each other warm.
The animals in the woods, howling and growling,
while me and the folks smiling and clowning.
I'm on the tree looking in the sky
and see the twinkling stars,
glad to be out from them stanky ol' bars.
The trees are swaying and the kids are playing,
Grandma in the house cookin' and bakin'.
It's a beautiful night and the family is tight.
We all goin' to stay up all night until the moon goes down
and the sun comes up
and shines his light.

Daniel A., 18

Hummingbirds

A cloud dreamily watched
angry helicopters
zoom by with crazy speed.

The ocean was ticklish
with fish and sea creatures
moving like a motor in her stomach.

The jail felt guilty
while humans used his teeth
for bars.

The pond
was lovestruck by the moon
looking down on him every night.

The flowers felt playful
under the touch
of the hummingbirds.

Huu Viet Chau, 14

I Remember Ukraine

I REMEMBER the fish
that my friends and family always caught.
I used to put them back in the lake
where we got them from because I felt sorry
for the poor little fishes.

I REMEMBER the markets
where my grandma and I used to always go
to buy chickens, rabbits, and kittens.

I REMEMBER the birch trees
that we always saw whenever we got to our street.

I REMEMBER the builders
building the big houses that took ten years to build.
All the time my friends and I used to go and play
in those unfinished buildings.

I REMEMBER the cold windy snow
pushing me back when I was trying to go forward.

Anna Zaytseva, 12

Mexico

Mexico reminds me of my tío's fruit trees.
Mexico reminds me of hot sun
    burning the dirty streets.
Mexico reminds me of loud barking dogs,
    fat pigs, and chickens.
Mexico reminds me of donkeys
    and pretty black horses.
It reminds me of my cousins
    and all the time we spend talking when I visit.
Mexico reminds me of eating
    that spicy menudo with extra cow skin.
Mexico reminds me of the brown eagle
    in the center of the Mexican flag.

Alejandra Gamez, 14

In Chinatown

Chinatown at night is as quiet as a temple.
But in the morning and afternoon
it is very noisy, like a flea market.
Then at evening, it's so quiet again.
In Chinatown I smell apples
and every kind of fish.
I feel Chinatown wants to be a zoo
because it has so many animals:
turtle, rabbit, butterfly, mouse, and duck.
Everyone looks so happy,
like on their birthday.
In Chinatown I can listen to people speak
Chinese. I can understand them.

And then I am happy to be in Chinatown.

De Feng Yu, 15

Searching for the Perfect Wave

Sitting on the rough board,
velcro from the wet suit burning.
Waiting, bobbing, glaring at the swells.
Waves come from storms from
faraway places.
The continual crashing of the waves,
the skin of my toes is like ice.

The swell becomes
a wave;
it shoots up like a bullet.
My reflexes sharp,
I align with the wave,
paddle for shore
with one thing in mind:
the ride,
the brisk wind drying my hair,
the crashing wave chasing me,
the feel of walking on water.

Jonathan Hansen-Weaver, 14

Jamaica

I'm in Jamaica
eating goat &
fishballs &
listening to
music. People
by the dock &
people behind
buildings with
drums saying
good morning
good afternoon
and good night.

Sharina Weatherspoon, 11

Sweet Mangoes

Philippines reminds me
of sinigang and lumpias,

sweet mangoes and my grandma's
good cooking,

my auntie who owns a candy store
and gave me gum,

Manila, the capital,
and my brother who took me to the mall.

Philippines reminds me of a young me.
I was skinny then.

Emmanuel Caramat, 12

El Salvador

I remember when my grandmother
was cooking,
oh the taste of tortillas!

I remember the feeling of the curtains
touching my face
and the smell of the clean air.
So beautiful in the morning
to wake up and breathe the clean air!

I remember the sight of my grandfather
angry with me,
making me scared.

I remember the sound of the beautiful river
when my family went swimming.
I miss all of this,
because here the city is too big,
and my country is very small.

Claudia Portillo, 18

Deep Inside

The best place I ever was is in my mind.
My body has never been there but my soul has.
When I go to this place I'm all alone.
It's a place of peace and tranquility
where I take time to grow.
The only problem that I have with this place
is that I can't stay long because of all the distractions
in front of my face.
This is like me because it's inside of me.
I go there whenever I have time to think.
This place is the best place I've ever been
because I can go there no matter where I'm at,
even in the pen. And this is the end...

Antoine, 17

It Is the Earth's Birthday

It is the earth's birthday today
and red-breasted robins soar through the lush green
tropical rainforests of Africa once again.

It is the earth's birthday today
and the heavens shatter,
releasing rain
on the hot deserts of Saudi Arabia.
This rain mixes with golden sands
to create the pot
that grows the five pillars of Islam.

It is the earth's birthday today
and the melting ice caps on the peaks
of the Himalayas
nourish the street children of India
bathing and soothing
their dry, cracked skin.

It is the earth's birthday today
and golden sunflowers rise
from the dirt roads of Kabul.

It is the earth's birthday today
and 40 sunken nuclear submarines
stop releasing deadly radiation
by the blue magic of mermaids
turning them into a school of silver fish
fluttering away into a city
of ruby coral.

It is the earth's birthday today
and green killing machines
withdraw their position outside of Palestine,
and the dead rise to life again
to eat a plate of chicken Kabob
with their family.

It is the earth's birthday today
and habitats of endangered species
are being destroyed by the clear cutting
of green trees at the borders
of the Amazon River.
But these animals hide
within their dark caves
of warm, underwater springs
to continue their survival.

It is the earth's birthday today
and large, golden bells ring with joy,
calling out the return
of ancient temples of Tibet,
once wiped out by the hatred of Buddhism.

It is the earth's birthday today
and the earth is standing on its knees,
worrying and crying deeply,
deeply about the fact that it is being renewed
by the wise, watery words of poetry.

Shahid Minapara, 14

Rander, India

Where I'm from
women bargain with merchants
from underneath their veils,
not taking no for an answer and threatening
to walk away.
And little children
with their mothers in the market
chase baby lambs.

Where I'm from you can hear the sound
of the Azan,
the soft voice calling people to prayer,
from anywhere.
At the sound of the Azan, women cover
their heads with their dupatas,
pausing all conversations
and men rush to the nearest mosque
for their daily prayers,
leaving anything and everything behind.

Where I'm from men sit after dinner
on cement porches, talking away the night
until their wives call for them.
And women at home gossip
while cutting almonds for tomorrow's dessert.

Where I'm from little girls in their dupatas
and little boys in their topies
run to the mosque for their praying lessons.
Rush through their Arabic alphabets
so they can go out and play.

Where I'm from sweet baraf golas
are made of ice and brightly colored syrups.
With baraf golas in their hands, young guys
and girls flirt with each other while their mothers
are exchanging biryani recipes.

Where I'm from my whole family
is in the living room at night
watching the latest Salman Khan movie
eating my aunt's warm roasted nuts.

Asefa Subedar, 16

Ireland

Today
I wake up and hear
the birds singing.
My grandma calls it
the dawn chorus.

Then I hear my sister
calling,
"Wait for me!"

Sara Aylward-Brown, 7

The Peacefulness of Mexico

I have my mother's brown eyes
                     and long hands.

I have my father's energy,
long legs
        and short fingers.

I have my grandmother's black hair.

I have my grandfather's energy and loneliness.

I have my aunt's caring thoughts.

I have the nature of a tiger.

And I have the peacefulness of Mexico.

         Ruben Cuevas, 17

Gifts of Life

I will give to my grandma a beautiful star
so she remembers me when she sees the star.

I will send to my sister the happiness
when we were together.

I will give to my brother half of my heart
so I will always be with him.

I will give to my mother my good wishes
so she knows I care for her.

I will give to my dad the wind
so when he feels it he will know I love him.

I will give to my husband all my life
so he will be happy.

I will give my children my caring, my love
so they can be good people in the future.

I will give all people the love in the world
so they can live with love in their hearts.

Gilma De León, 18

Ramadan

For Ramadan I will give something nice
to my mother,
some new clothes so she will be happy
with me,
and before she goes back home to our country
I will give her some money for my sister.

I will give my father some new clothes also.
Then I'll give my friends the happiness
and memories of when we were all together.
No one will feel lonely.

I'm giving my brother a new car
because he is nice to me,
he drives me around in this country
in his taxi.

I'm sending my grandfather
something to drink in the hospital
in my country
before he dies.

Abd Hammash, 15

Where I Want to Be

Where I am from
birds nest on a tree,
kids come out to play
and trip on their feet.

I see the colors around me,
a rainbow is what I see,
looking at my sister dancing
on the street,
what I see is my home,
and that is where I want to be.

Gabriel Deras, 12

Aja Cayetano

A young latin warrior who flies like the wind,
a goddess of the birds. A speaker of justice
and pride.
This latin warrior is full of spirit that flows
like butterflies in the wind, flying away
from the harms and the dangers of the night
speed blowing breeze.
A goddess of the birds, she is soft and swift
as she moves against the wind in the lightly shaded
sky. She moves her wings up and down from
side to side in perfect harmony with the sounds
of the still life that surrounds her.
With the words of justice and her voice
sounding like Pride, she dives
into the crowd screaming, "The life
I live is my life, not yours, let my
voice ring out to the sea.
I love my Raza heritage."

Aja Cayetano, 16

My Mommy

My mommy who dresses in her best clothes
for a party,
who gives me what I want,
who cooked her best curry for us,
who worries about me
when I am sick in my small bed,
who is angry when I make mistakes
with my little brother,
who cried when she left her own country,
who really wants a beautiful diamond ring
she saw in the shop,
who is very lovely
when she buys me a beautiful dress,
who calls me
My Beautiful Sweetheart.

Ei Ei Kyu San, 15

When I Grow Up

When I grow up, I want to remember
how much I loved to tie my short hair
with a beautiful ribbon,
or tear off the paper of the calendar,
how scared I was of ants that crawled toward me slowly,
how much I hated that the babysitter asked me to sleep
when I was full of vitality,
what fun it was to draw pictures on the wall with crayons,
to fold a paper airplane and fly it.

Yan Jun Xu, 15

You Bring Out the Latino in Me

inspired by Sandra Cisneros' "You Bring Out the Mexican in Me"

You bring out the Latin culture in me
the mariachi in me
the marimba in me
the pupusas Salvadorenos in me
You bring out the September 15th in me
the Latin spitfire in me
The capoeira in me
the eagle, Quetzal and freedom in me
The guanacos, chapines and Aztecas in me
the love por mi tierra Latino in me
The enchiladas, empanadas and tacos in me
You bring out the Maya in me
The amor in me
You, only you, bring out all this in me
You, only you, Latin America
bring out all this in me

Erick Piedrasanta, 16

Today I Feel

Today I feel like a blooming flower
in the sun,
like a leaf getting ready to fall from a tree
when the seasons change.
I feel clean and fresh
like water and oceans in summer time,
like a bird, free and let loose.
I don't even know what to do.
I'm an egg getting ready to hatch
from a nest,
a baby bird ready to fly,
a star shining so bright,
so peaceful in the night.

Remy Stapleton, 13

New York Sites

New York is a city of peace.
The Statue of Liberty represents freedom
and world peace.
New York is a city of buildings
and different peoples.
After the terrorist attack in New York
everyone learned that this world
needs peace and freedom.
In New York's Central Park
everyone who lives in New York
goes to Central Park to relax.
When you go to Central Park
the air is so fresh,
same with the grass.
Behind the trees
there goes the tall buildings.
That's what New York is.

Bella Tishkovskaya, 11

Indian Spirit

As I lie in my bed
I listen to the spirits
that wander at night.
Suddenly I hear my grandma's voice
calling for me.
I open my eyes
seeking her like an owl
stalking his prey.
But I don't see her.
My eyes get watery
and tears start flowing like rivers.
I picture her in my head,
her black hair,
her brown skin,
representing the great Indian
that she was.

Octavio S., 19

I Remember

I remember the sight
of the gray of the clouds
in winter and the
waterfall in Guacamayas.

I remember the sound
of my mother's voice
when she screamed to
me in the dark,
"It's time to go to school."

I remember the taste
of the enchiladas
when the festival
started in the square.

I remember the smell
of the wet soil
when it started to
rain in Michoacán.

I remember the touch
of the hard hands
of my tired father
when he returned
from the farm.

Ignacio Sandoval, 16

The Other Side

When you look out at the freeway,
you might see cars,
but I see rainbow lights
scattering this way and that.

When you look out at the city,
you might see buildings and houses,
but I see a magical and peaceful place.

When you look out your window,
you might see a dirty bus,
but I see toys
dancing off the walls and seats.

Kali Shelton, 11

Why I Love Aú

When I do aú
I feel like I am flying
and as I fly, I grin.

When I do aú
I feel like a bird in the air
and as I fly in the air I sing a sweet tweet.

I spin and grin
and it makes me
feel like the wind.

When I sing the music
I feel the movement.

When I get dizzy and tired
my teacher says,
"Come on, guys, let's be admired!"

I don't give up because I love aús.
Aús can be blue, but I love it.
Put power in yourself.

Angelica Pineda, 8

Aú is a move in the Brazilian martial art of capoeira that closely resembles a cartwheel.

Rain

How magical favorite nature
falls in the small
drops from clouds in the sky.
It's so beautiful.
I feel comfortable and romantic
when I walk in the raining day without any umbrella
it's like my grandmother's hands touch me
when it falls on my face and hands.
It looks like a wonderful dancer
when it falls
on the leaves of the trees and the ground.
It listens like a great love song
when it falls
on the iron roofs like the beating of drums.
It's rain!

Minny Wang, 18

Coconut Milk

Sunset turns the blue sky
into red, purple, and orange.
Small, warm breezes lift
the hair out of your face.
Palm trees cover your surroundings.
You just sit in your chair
looking into the sun and listening
to the water splash against the sand.

A coconut falls and breaks open.

You see the white inside, the sparkling milk.
You think of the white meat before the coconut opened.

It was caged in the coconut darkness
with the memory of its ancestors,
used to manufacture grease
for our people's hair.

One coconut brother was sold
to an old woman.
She drinks its milk now
with such a refreshing feeling,
then closes her eyes and wishes
to be with you
on that beach,
thinking and thinking.

Rigoberto Canchola, 13

15th Street

My grandmother who
lives on 15th Street,
who cries when
she goes to church,
who hugs me good-night,
who is my right hand.

Armando Aguilar, 12

House of Dreams

In the house of dreams
there are pictures on the wall
that smile at me
when I wake up in the morning.

Through the ceiling
I can communicate
with my dead family members.

Sometimes my grandmother
sits on the stairs
drinking her coffee
the way she used to do.

The fireplace flames up
with memories of my life,
a magical TV of dreams.

The cabinets open
if I ask them to,
and birds are free to fly
all about the house.

Reygen Pardilla, 13

My Mom

Her arms are two doors I go in
so she can give me a hug.
She is a cherry on the cherry
tree I planted.
Her lips are two apples that I eat.
Her laugh is like the wind
blowing in front of me.

Samantha Cortez, 9

The Seasons Back Home

I remember Spring,
our garden flowers opening,
butterflies and bees circling.

I remember Summer,
our pond giving up its water to the Sun,
a sweet rain filling it up again.

I remember Fall,
our garden flowers gone,
the tree leaves changing clothes,
green becoming yellow and orange.

I remember Winter,
our pond giving its water to the thirsty earth,
just some small fish in the pond.

I am smiling
full of memories.

Zhen Wen Zhang, 17

My Brother

My brother's name is Avery.
When he sleeps, he sounds like a foghorn.
His head is shaped like a big orange.
His nose is as big as a small peach.
My brother's love is stronger than a blizzard.
I love my brother and my brother loves me
and that can never change.

Grace Sizelove, 9

Monkey

I have a monkey
inside of me
because I like bananas
and I'm wild.

When somebody
calls me names about my hair
my monkey tells me
to ignore it.

Angel Allen, 10

Night and Day

In China
the night is warm
the sky has many stars
and a big moon.
In the city I hear families laugh
the insects singing
and the music
slow moving.

Morning in the market
I smell the flowers fragrant
and candies sweet
the mango the watermelon.
I see many colors of ice cream
many packs of chips
and people crowding in
to buy them.

Liu-Fen Zeng, 16

My Heart

My heart is like a strawberry,
a lion roaring,
like a sunflower dancing in the grass.
My heart is beeping like the sun,
moving like the water.
My heart is wiggling like a fish.

Tommy Nguyen, 8

The Reflection of My Eyes

I am like the ocean sea,
so beautiful and caring,
so peaceful and grateful,
just like water roaming with fish,
and so many things just going through the water,
making my eyes glimmer like they were diamonds.

Jesse Paul Meek, 10

five

HOPE WAITS, LIKE US

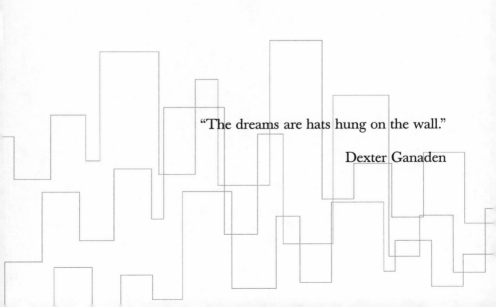

"The dreams are hats hung on the wall."

Dexter Ganaden

Uttarayan, Festival of the Kites
Ahmadabad, India

In the blink of an eye
wingless birds overpower the skies,
beautiful combinations of colors
arise in the thousands of kites
that soar the low heaven.

On this day winter is over and summer has begun.
The sun continues its drift toward the highest throne.
All of India's men, women, and children stand upon their roofs,
Muslim beside Hindu, Christian beside Sikh,
connecting their minds to the red and white
dragonflies darting in sharp angles above.

Countless numbers of heads look up all day,
praising the sun
for releasing its warmth upon their faces.

Every string is painted with tiny glass shards
so that the paths might cross in playful battle,
cutting the strings and releasing the kites to the wind.
Street children run like wild beasts
to catch the fallen kites and sell them for one rupee.

The innocent pleasure of this festival
spells its name across the faces of rickshaw drivers,
factory workers, and doctors,
each laughs and smiles open-mindedly,
knowing there is no work today or tomorrow.

As the day comes to an end, pollution begins to rise
in clouds of blooming flowers, a dull finishing of red.
The sun slowly drowns into the ocean
in sheets of blue flame.

Shahid Minapara, 15

Sleep

The windows are blue.
The colorful moonlight
shines on the blue glass,
and you can see through the doors.

The dreams are hats
hung
on
the
wall.

Dexter Ganaden, 13

The Healing

With my healing hands I will cure
every disease in the world,
so people won't have to worry.

With my healing hands I will erase
racism, prejudice, and sexism,
turn them into three more stars
in the sky.

Susana Sandoval, 13

Hope Sounds Like the Sea

Hope is dark blue.
Hope sounds like the sea
waiting for emotions of waves
which will break on the rocks
making a sound like a splash.

Hope feels like staying in one place
where you will wait forever,
wait forever
like a tree or a volcano.

Hope smells like pure love
like a bunch of red roses
for someone special who knows
everything about you.

Hope tastes like a word called loneliness
showing and saying
I'm going to wait for you 4ever.

Hope looks like a shape,
a shape of something impossible to move
or break
like a lake or a mountain.

Hope is like me because it waits.
I wait, I wait,
and I wait for you
because you are worth it.

Raudel Ruiz May, 18

Equality

Equality means when an Iraqi travels
from Iraq to America
they don't get sent back
to their country
because the police
think they are a terrorist.

Equality means when a Latino
has a new car
and he doesn't get arrested
because the police thinks
he sold drugs to buy the car.

Equality means when teenagers
have the freedom to go into a club
without the owner thinking
they are going to drink alcohol.

Equality means
when a woman
is president
of the United States
for once.

Valentina Prado, 14

Dragon in Eagle's House

I am Chinese living in the United States.
Chinese is the offspring of dragon.
I am the offspring of dragon.
Dragon means powerful and elitist.
I have no power in the U.S.
Eagle is more powerful than dragon
because this is eagle's house.
Eagle doesn't treat dragon well
because dragon is going to grab eagle's food.
But dragon won't grab eagle's food.
Dragon will help the eagle build its land.

Fu Xiong Zeng, 19

Anger

Anger lives in a lonely cave
where he even gets mad at the bats
for making noises while he is sleeping.

He wears a shawl around his shoulders,
sits on rocks, and spits in a bucket,
talking to himself because he's lonely.

He has black eyes, a fierce face,
red hands, and crooked yellow teeth,
with a mouth scrumped up into a grrrrrr.

Anger does not have a wife
because he does not want to be responsible
for someone else,
so he scares them away.

Anger dreams of having friends,
not always being cruel and nasty,
but when hope flutters by his window
he closes the curtains.

Saman Minapara, 9

One Body Found by Love

Violence seeps through our society
like a cracked wall,
drenching us with ignorance and hate.

Peace seems like a forgotten jewel
in a red boiling ocean
waiting to be found by love.

Our days sink deeper into sorrow
and death awaits us like a mournful ghost
waiting in the shadows.
9/11 was one of those days
that stuck with us like a splinter
that can't be removed,
and screams and cries
can still be heard inside our hearts.

But Dr. King had a dream
that carried us through good and bad.
Dr. King had a dream that peace would materialize
into reality,
that bigotry would be just a memory,
that one day we could look past
skin color and differences,
that all cultures would be treasured.

And that every drop of blood
spilled from our ancestors,
would fit in one vein, one body,
to make a difference.

Evangelina Thomas-Guevara, 13

My Feelings

Inside me is a sun,
shining and shining on everyone.
Inside me is a bird, flying and soaring.
Inside me is a snake.
It makes me mad and it rattles
to let you know when you're too close.
Inside me is a tree, tall and shady.
Inside me is a dying flower.
I get sadder and sadder.
Inside me is the sky.
I hold it inside.
I won't let thunder roar.

Inside me is a heart that is dancing.

Denise Navarro, 8

My Imagination

Choi Wa Kuong,
honest, helpful and nice,
who dreams that I am a star in the sky
who wishes everyone will love each other and be happy
who fears my friends and family will leave me
who wants to be successful in the future

who will explore Japan to learn
who enjoys going outside with my family
    and talking with my friends
who wonders why we have war in the world
who believes in timeless love and friendship

who hopes my family and friends believe me
who loves all of my friends and family
who plans my life that I want to have
who imagines that maybe we can live on Mars

who will pray for everyone
who will listen and help friends solve problems
who will laugh that I hope
    tomorrow will be better

      Choi Wa Kuong, 17

My Brother

My brother is a bamboo pole.
Sometimes I am jealous of him.
He always eats too much, but he's never fat.
Also, his skin is better than mine.

Sometimes I hate him.
His smile is very fake, but
when he laughs it is a loudspeaker.
He is shy, so when he has some questions,
he always asks me to ask other people.
So, many people think that I am older than him.
"No! I am his younger sister!" That's what I always say.
When we were young, we often fought,
and I always got hurt and I was angry. Now,
I've grown up. We never fight, but
we always dispute.

Sometimes I love him so much, but
I've never told him.
He's kind to me.
I like his fried rice, which is delicious.
Maybe one day, I will say to him,
"I love you, my brother! My only one!"

Zhi Min Lin, 16

Abuelita Birra

Who's Abuelita Birra?

Is she that Pink Rose who gave birth to my mother?

Is Abuelita Birra that Pink Rose
who has mariposas, claveles, árboles de naranjas in her garden?

Who every day at five in the morning wakes up
and gets her hose and regando las plantas?

Who's Abuelita Birra?

That Rosada Rosa, every time a grandchild is born,
a new rose blooms
in her garden.

People in the morning see her in her flowered dress and
guaraches
clipping the dead roses, feeding the living ones.

When the sun comes out, it always comes to that beautiful
Pink Rose's house.

Lizzeth Carmona, 15

Counting the Ways

My family is a blessing
when we are yelling
at the top of our lungs,
fighting and arguing and being the loudest Mexicans on the
block.

My family is a blessing when we all get together
on Easter and crack flour eggs on each other's heads.

My family is a blessing when we all get together
and go delirious, act stupid and laugh till our stomachs hurt
and we're crying, in tears.

My family is a blessing when we get together
for special events,
like to plan my sista's baby shower.

My family is a blessing when after seeing a scary movie
like *The Blair Witch Project*
Tina wants to sleep in my room.

My family is a blessing when someone wants
to borrow money from you.

My family is a blessing when my cousin
wanna whip on her baby's daddy.

My family is a blessing when we have
our Mother/Daughter Days or Sister Days.

My family is a blessing when we say goodbye
to each other, we always cry.

My family is a blessing 'cause,
damn, I have a big family!

My family is a blessing when me and my sister
get on my Dad's nerves.

My family is a blessing 'cause there's no other family
like my family.

Andrea Rodriguez, 21

My Magic Senses

With my hands I can feel
the softness of my pillow
made of cotton.
It is my comfort,
my joy and happiness after
the times of sadness.

With my magic hands I can touch
and reach my dreams,
I can fly as high as the clouds
and the birds,
I can touch the stars and moon above.

With my eyes I can see
my fellows. I can see the children
playing and having fun. I can see myself
playing in the sand.

With my magic eyes I can see
the sadness of people's past,
the horrible things
that have saddened them,
the good things that inspired them
and made them happy.

Steffanie Surga La Cumbis, 14

The Tree

The tree of my mind
is happy and healthy when it is being loved
and cared for.
The roots suck up the love
to feed the leaves, trunk, and animals.

The birds in the tree are the voices inside,
which respond to my questions.
The owl is the tree's lookout while I sleep.

The monkeys in the tree
represent my craziness.
They swing from branch to branch,
screaming and playing different games.

The squirrel in my mind
collects food for the tree during winter.

When my mom hugs me, I am filled with joy,
and my mind sprouts flowers,
yellow and pink with green stems
to represent life and sunshine.

When my sister died
the tree became bare with nothing on it.

But when spring came again,
my tree grew new leaves.

Cierra Crowell, 9

Nani

She is the bright orange,
orange as the evening sun.
She smells like the early morning breeze.
She is the soft sound of clattering dishes
when they are being washed.
She moves slowly through the long narrow balcony,
one step carefully at a time.
She sits by the window reading the Koran
with her cat, Manju, next to her,
brushing her fur through Nani's feet.
She wears a thin white salwar kamiz
with tiny blue flowers and lacey lace,
plain white pants with a nylon ordni
that goes on her head, loops around her neck
with the end hanging down her chest.
Her feet are covered with thin rubber chappals
that clap against her feet each time she walks.
She has a tiny purse with crisp rupees and coins
and the key to the house that she tucks in her bra strap
with a pink handkerchief called a ramal.
In her nose, she wears a big flowerlike nose pin

with red and white rubies.
She dreams about the day
that we will come back from school in Bombay,
where I live with my parents and other grandma.
She dreams about filling
the basketlike jars that hang from the ceiling
with freshly made butter biscuits
bought from the store by the river.
She will say, "Jali gahri aha,"
Come home early.

Asefa Subedar, 14

No Mo

No Mo drama in the streets,
'cause nobody can kill without no heat.
Guns, knives, and other stuff is gone,
computers that turn into phones,
cars that hover up in the air,
racist people is nowhere.

Cops are not violent but nice,
everybody go together like beans and rice.
Gun smoke though is still in the sky,
little kids got toys that make them fly,
nobody cries no mo, and the white house is red,
nobody goes to war, nobody comes up dead.
We all live in peace together,
look up in the sky and it's always sunny weather,
nobody is smokin' cause it's no trees to blow,
that's what it would look like if bad was No Mo.

Antoine Johnson, 13

Freedom

I will love and cherish freedom more
By making something of myself
Doing positive things that benefit others
Sit down and talk to the younger generations
About what they are headed for
I will kiss freedom every morning
I will tell freedom that I love him
I will tell him on unexpected occasions
Freedom awaits

Occupying myself to do right is a need
So I am focused
And not dazed by freedom
Freedom is for the ones who want it
People yearn for as many rights as they have in Log Cabin
I'm lucky
And I want Freedom

Hardy H., 17

Stories of Our Past

The house of the mind is a peaceful place,
where the walls tell a story.
The front door has a picture of Muhammad Ali,
the world's greatest boxer.
Going up the stairs to enter the dining room
you see the great kings
of our past.

Some doors are open,
some doors are locked.
The locked doors have stories to tell us
that we're not ready for.

In the attic are all the constellation signs,
like Capricorn, Gemini, Aries,
Leo, Taurus. Pisces.
They tell the story
of what it means to be born during that time
and what other sign is a good match.

But in the basement
are horrible urban legends.
That's why there's no door
to get in or out of the basement.

In the house of the mind
there's a room
with thousands of African-American pictures
telling stories
like Dr. King saying,
I Have A Dream
when thousands of people
came to listen.
There's Rosa Parks, C.J. Walker,
George Washington Carver,
Jackie Robinson &
Harriet Tubman,
each telling their story.

But down the hall past the princes,
kings, queens and princesses of Egypt,
there's a small room
somewhat back like a closet.
In the small room
is a bigger door
that leads to a room with white,
fluffy clouds,
and inside of the clouds
you can see your future.

Marshay Dillard, 13

I Want to Send

a plastic frog to Mr. Zapien
because he likes 'em.

a better school to Ms. Hernandez
because she needs one really bad.

a garden to my grandma
because she loves plants.

color pencils
and everything an artist needs
to my uncles
so they'll paint this world peaceful.

more money to El Salvador
so that there won't be more sadness.

my neighbors happiness
because their dog died two years ago.

Michelle a large big room
so that she could teach us
in a private room just for her.

a letter to myself
so that I could remember
when I was a child.

Carlos Cartagena, 12

WAR

WAR
You are going too FAR
STOP
We got to MOP UP
This mess man,
This feels like a test.

Together we can fix this,
Don't use fists,
It is just going to make things worse,
We can talk first.

Don't send our girls and boys,
You are acting like they are toys,
Don't take the war that far,
We can fix this mess,
But remember,
Be careful,
Cause this is not a test.

Bianca Porras, 10

The Bus to the Big House

It seemed like I grew up in the middle of the night,
because where I'm from there is no light.

I never go nowhere wit'out havin' a fight,
I guess that's because we have unequal rights.

Young homies don't tell me that the light
they shine in our faces is too bright,
because it's easy to see they're tryin'
to put us away for life.

Nowdayz we just doin' anything,
tryin' to earn these stripes,
but we gon' keep thinkin' it's cool until
they hit us with that third strike.

So before we make that move,
let's take a moment to think twice.
Because they ain't playin' no mo',
they throwin' us in the pen,
especially if we ain't white.

Don't wait fa no bus ta go ta San Quentin,
let's take a vacation,
let's take a flight.
They love seeing us kill each other,
so let's get together
and re-unite.

Leo P., 17

Something to Live For

Silence sweeps the room.
I can feel the fire,
the fiery rage
that makes me think shady.
I know I should go calm myself down.
I know my peace has to come
from looking in the eyes of my newborn baby.
So I sit with her by the window
and watch the stray dogs play on the hillside.

If I didn't have my baby girl
I might go insane.
When I think about her
I think about life,
and there goes the sound of a passing train.

Onnie B., 19

The Ghetto

The ghetto is a place
where nothing's ever mellow
where people say, "What's up?"
instead of saying hello.

Where the poor and the lost grow cold
where guns are shot and drugs are sold
where the cats chase the rats
and the dogs chase them all
from the crack in the sacks
to the macks tryna ball
tennis shoes on the phone pole
spray paint on the wall
laughing children with snotty noses
and stains in their drawers
mothers on welfare
three kids gotta share
two sleep in the bed
the other in the chair.

Underneath there's suffering, hurting, real pain
on the streets it's occurring, minds twirling insane
for the fiends with the addictions
their life is a shame
scream at their children
their wife is to blame
they want it so much
they'll do anything for cocaine
they're on it so much
they forget their own name.

You can run, but can't hide
only some escape
some sold drugs and bought their way out
some showed love and fought their way out
some played hoops and shot their way out
some rapped a demo and hip-hopped their way out
some found family and thought their way out.

But one day, everything will be all settled
one day, maybe one day
everyone will be cool in the ghetto.

       Neil B., 17

Nigeria's Girls

To me, I am what I am.
I know from whence I came.
I am Nigerian.

When I think back to where I came from.
All I see is the long walk there.
The long walk to my father's village and my own.

Life as Nigerian is hard.
Not many of us come to America.
Not many of us girls see what I see.
Nigerian girls are lost.

They are lost when they step
    foot on the free land of America.
I'm not saying that they hate life
here or like it.
But all I know is when they
    step off that plane or boat,
    they may never go back.

You know how they say, "You
can't teach a dog a new trick"?

You can never take a good
    girl away from her life.
Nigeria's girls say they
    want change
But can you change from whence you came?
Can you still be proud?
I am the voice of many!
I am a Nigerian girl!
I see the sun rise each morning
    and set each evening.
I am the leader of tomorrow
    because I know I am one of
    Nigeria's girls, today.

        Ibukun Hambolu, 16

This Is What I Want to Pass On

My dearest child,
you are all I have. A beautiful child.
My beautiful child.

My days are finite. I won't be around forever
so to you I leave:

A JOURNEY—
      sleep laugh play dream learn

A QUEST—
      Look within yourself and
      grow to love what you see.

A PASSION—
      Your work on this planet is far from over.
Use your voice and your power
to change our sullen world.

WHEN I GO—
      Take my smile—replicate it.
      Feel my soul—hold it close.

      Lateefah Simon, 22

Mother Who

Mother who didn't like a messy house,
especially her own,
who was always helping me work hard.

My mother, who used to make chicken soup
for anyone who had a cold,
who bought me a soccer ball
when she saw I liked soccer.

My mother, who tries not to cry
whenever she talks to her father
in Morocco on the phone,

who is always preparing delicious meals
for my father when he gets back from work,

who decided to leave her parents
and come to the United States with us
because she wants us to have a better future.

Elmehdi Rahmaoui, 15

Anthem to the Tree of Freedom

From a seed to a strong, mighty tree,
there stands the Tree of Freedom.
From Martin Luther King's
"I have a dream!"
to Rosa Parks fighting
for the front of that bus,
we will forever stand with no fear inside
because God shall be with us!

The tears we've shed day and night,
the words we've prayed to keep our faith,
the lives that were taken shall not rest in peace.
The hopes that have fallen pick us up,
and we believed,
we believed this seed
would grow to freedom!

Indeed, yes! We will forever stand, no fear inside
because God shall be with us.
Those who have died shall still remain here inside
because of their mighty pride.

Indeed, yes! We shall overcome someday.
We shall walk hand in hand,
no more sorrow in our hearts.
We shall forever stand,
saying, "That path was dark, but now I'm free!"
No more chains will remain.
No more people getting hanged.
No more sacks on our backs.
No more suffering through pain.
No more sisters getting raped.
No more picking cotton in the rain.
No more lives being taken.
All our lives will change!

Because of our faith,
because we believed that the seed
would grow to freedom and forever stand,
the Tree of Freedom!

Qiana Powell, 14

Where My Beauty Comes From

I have my mother's eyes
and my father's sensitivity.
I have my gramma's smile
and my grandmother's high, proud cheekbones.
I have my granpa's words
and my grandfather's light brown skin.
I have my aunt's smart mouth
and my cousin's dark magenta lips.
I have my uncle's humor
and my cousin-brother's style.
I have my own intelligence, which
I shall pass down to my own child.

Sadaf Minapara, 14

Blessing

May it snow in San Francisco.
May the fishes talk to you.
May the sharks not eat people.
May the homeless have houses.
May you sleep in the clouds.
May your heart beat like a song.
May people not sweat in the summer.
May you swim in spaghetti.
May you travel in space.
May people not drown.
May your clothes glow in the dark.
When you get cut, may you not bleed.
May yams turn to hams.
May you be able to pick up a table with one finger.
May there be no guns.
May your world be full of shiny crystal pearls.
May your heart come out and see heaven.

Mercy Services Group Poem

Work for Change

for the Rev. Martin Luther King Jr.

You worked for people of color,
died for your great work.
We will remember you forever.
Now people of color have more power than before.
"Whites Only" sign,
no longer on the restaurant's door.
We can sit on any seat on the bus.
Even the mayor of San Francisco is not a White man.

Of course there is not total equality.
The White people and the rich
may look down on the colored and poor.
The United States is changed but still is unfair.
People from other countries do not
have as much power as people born here.
We have a lot of work to do to make all people equal.

Penelope Zheng, 17

I Wish

I wish that everyone would live in peace.
I wish that there would be no more school shootings.
I wish that everyone would be smart and go far in life.
I wish that there would be no more kidnapping and murder.
I wish that everyone would live in happiness.
I wish no one would call me names.
I wish that people would respect one another.
I wish that kids would have a voice in this world.
I wish that people would not judge others by their color
    and how they look.
That's what I wish.

Whitney Spencer, 12

Healer of Natoma

I. THE HEALED
Healer of Natoma
can feel the person's pain.
In his mind, he sees
images of the
person, he can feel
the pain in his heart.

Walking in the woods,
he appears to me
as my aid.
He kneels beside me
as he stretches his arm.
Flow of white light
pours into my heart.

II. MR. EPIDEMIC
A life in a sewer and
an enemy that cures.
"I hate it all," I would say.
I laugh that my breath
of air and poison
makes a flower die
from its living life.
I love my germs. Cruelty.
Bias. Despair. I love to
spread them out to the world.

III. THE HEALER'S MOTHER AND FATHER
They love their son,
only he's a teenager.

"He may get A's but he's very
unusual and silent
within," the parents say.
The parents always talk about
the son during the night.
"Maybe friends," the father says.
"For what he is,
he's still our little
boy. He's kind of unusual,
but we still love him."

IV. HEALER OF NATOMA
I am a healer
with your love
to the world and others,
in your heart they
work both ways.

My love goes to the world and others.

Our hope may break
like a broken vase,
but the soul is
filled with joy.

The temple is our soul.
For that we are
beautiful in other ways.

If you help others,
your soul is kind.

Vicente Nalam, 14

The Sweater

A sweater washed away by the rain
settled near a front porch
where an old woman lived.

When the sun rose
the woman came out and found the sweater
and took it inside.

She said to herself
that the sweater had sheltered other people
from the harsh weather of the past,
so she washed and fixed it.

The sweater came from the wool
of a sheep.
It warmed the sheep, she thought, and people too,
and many journeys carried the sweater to her.
Now the old sweater was ready
for another journey.

Jorge Pacheco, 13

Broken Man

The voice of a broken man brought to the
"Promise Land"
he never asked to be brought here but he
came out of fear
chains, whips, and slavery
stripped him of his bravery
when he was a man
broken from years of dedication
broken from the lack of education
broken from the lack of self-knowledge
and broken from the "white man's college"
people of America we need to get together
and share this land
and not end up like the broken man

Raeana Martin, 16

A Beautiful Painting

When I close my eyes,
I see the color black,
my hair.
I see people.
When I open my eyes,
I see my bedroom
in my real house.
I got dolls on my bed.

When I dream,
I see people talking
and lots of things
like backpacks, clothes,
shoes, games, and knockers.

When I paint,
I see the color yellow
and the shape of squares.
I take a picture of my cousins,
Carolyn, Nikki, Jaleshia, and Lakeiya,
and my friends, Keri and Iris.
I paint flowers and butterflies.

I see through the future:
my family
and what I am going to be
like an artist, teacher,
and veterinarian.
It will look like
a beautiful painting.

Nichelle Fullbright, 10

six

OURS POETICA

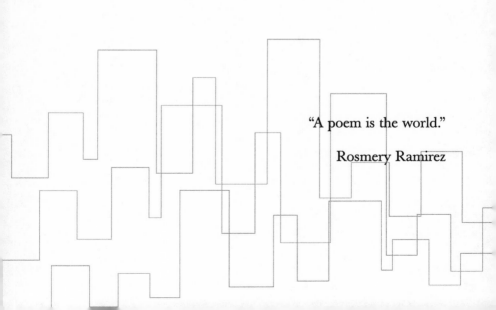

"A poem is the world."

Rosmery Ramirez

My Poem about Peace

Peace goes through my head every day,
but every day I see fights.
The fighting must cease,
fighting is wrong,
peace is cool.

The war in Iraq is wrong too,
but I can't stop the wars
because I'm a kid like you.

People work for peace every day.
So I crease my paper hoping for peace,
and we will not cease the marches
until the people have peace...

PEACE!!

       Nalashi Almendral, 9

How to Sing

First, you have to open your mouth
so you can let out a song
that will make the birds jealous enough
to crack the sky.

Make the song so beautiful
angels cry.

Sing 'til church bells ring.
Sing from the heart.
Sing, baby, sing.

Dannesha Nash, 12

Anything

Poetry is the story of the soul
vivid pictures
that pulse through our minds.

Pictures of the night sky
our fears
our living dreams.

The poetry
of beautiful things
dreadful things
anything.

Janudine (Tom) Tran, 13

The Music of Poetry

Poetry is like the colored leaves
that fall from the rusted trees in autumn.
Poetry is like a huge puzzle
that can always be put together in the right way
no matter if it does not make any sense at all.
Poetry is like the big, fat, orange cheesy moon
that the hairy grey wolves
sing their lullabies to.
The music of poetry
can be heard only at night when you think
you can't hear anything at all.

Cierra Crowell, 10

I Need to Write

I need to write
For those people who died
Under "tonton macoute" guns

The men went around to the Lycee
A boys' school
Brought the boys to Titanyen
To kill them

I need to write
For the bodies I saw in Titanyen
For the young men killed in Titanyen

I need to write
about their dead bodies
skin and bones that remind me of slaves
dying in the sugarcane fields

I need to write
For those young boys
Who had their heads hung

I need to write
For the red blood
Turned black

I need to write
For the blood
Floating in the Titanyan river

I need to write
Because those boys
Could not talk back

Emmanuela Ocean, 19

Everything

A poem is many Indians dancing
and singing. A poem is many birds
flying free. I
am
a poem.

A poem is a young Amazon girl.
She is sad. She is
the world.

A poem is a big cataract,
the water
coming down.

A poem is the people in the church
praying for peace
for everyone.

A poem is a question,
Why do people do bad things
in this beautiful world?

David Hernandez, 17

Poetry

Poetry is like my mom's
vase that just fell and
broke. I have to put
the pieces back together,
but they don't know where
they belong.

Jacqueline Beck, 10

The City

A poem is my city.
Massive vibrations in the street,
cars and trucks where people meet,
words create these.

City,
    surreal life,
living and knowing,
    an all-being of tall building dreams,
while people scream violence with words.

City,
this poem is my city
    where words form flowers of poetic violence
that flow creating showers of poetic silence.
    My city of words is like a peace movement
the U.S. government is afraid of.

I see my city painted artistically.
Beautiful murals shine every block,
    radiant beams of sunshine
light up antiwar demonstrations,
    where liberation is not bombs dropping
but true artistic freedom.
    Jail bars and pits of government tar,
unreal,
    this city is known to me.

Where fascist police don't roam the streets
    beating nightsticks of non-peace.

Where cars don't consume
    and sirens don't sound.
Are these the colors of liberation I've found?

My city is green redwoods shining in the sky,
birds and life flying high,
    solar power that's pollution free,
for this would truly liberate me.

    Where bombs don't fall creating acidic life,
can you see the fear in their eyes?
    Like shattered bricks on the floor,
how would you like a bomb on your front door?

    I can see him right now.
He's sitting on his comfortable chair of colonialism,
    stroking dark fingers of retaliation,
making sounds of effortless violence,
    intruding into peaceful lives of silence
that live to see death once more.

IS THIS THE LIBERATOR WE VOTED FOR?
IS THIS THE LIBERATOR WE VOTED FOR?

City.
    I see my city
painted artistically,
    changing things now so future generations
will see that we had a voice,
    and we took to the streets.

REVOLUTION NOW STARTS WITH YOU AND ME!
REVOLUTION NOW STARTS WITH YOU AND ME!
REVOLUTION NOW STARTS WITH YOU AND ME!

    Eric Cornforth, 16

Poetry Does Not Come Easy to Me

Poetry
does not come easy to me

Hard
that's the word
inspiration
that's what I need
poetry
that's what I love to write

For some it flows
like a mountain stream

For me
it's like moving a boulder on the sidewalk
with your bare hands
impossible
for most people

But
once in a while
that flower blooms
and my words are like a desert storm

Afterwards
it's calm
and my journey for words starts again

Ben Carter, 16

A Simple Piece of Nothing

Poetry can catch leaves
falling off the autumn trees.
Poetry should carry a small backpack
filled with infinitable knowledge.
Poetry should shop for those
who are not capable of doing so
and feed them by hand.
Poetry should be sharp
as the corner of a blade
that can catch flies with its eyes closed.
A business man walking, a homeless man sleeping,
a maid cleaning,
a lawyer arguing,
just a simple piece of nothing
that can fulfill the world's dreams.

Shahid Minapara, 15

What Poetry Is

Poetry should be a sweet sugar plum saying,
"Don't eat me, don't eat me."
Poetry should sing a sweet love song to the mirror.
Poetry should be a football being thrown by famous
    football stars.
Poetry should be a pen with no more ink.
Poetry should be magic thrown in the air and make
    wishes come true.
Poetry should be education for all the kids.
Poetry should be a lady at court during a trial.
Poetry should be a powerful world.
Poetry should be doing the normal thing.

    Bella Tishkovskaya, 11

The Girl Hidden

Poetry is the soft whispers
of the women gossiping in the living room.

She is the flowerpot
on the kitchen windowsill.

She is the sound of the radio
telling the daily news

and the forbidden tunes flying in the air.

She is the spices
being dropped in the boiling curry
sending a shocking smell to the hungry
men on the balcony.

Poetry is the girl
hidden underneath the bed
eating sweets from the plastic teacup.

She is the sneaky cat jumping
from roof to roof knocking
the clothes down from the clothesline.

Asefa Subedar, 15

How Poetry Feels

To wake up
on a bright, Saturday morning
with the smell of pancakes,
the day is like a wild animal.
You don't know what comes next.

Poetry is your bird.
The mind is free, and your pencil is alive.
Your thoughts pour
into the ocean of words.

Poetry feels like putting words
on paper with secret meanings
only you can understand.
When people read your poems
they give the words new meanings.

A poem is born
and passed around
to give light to others.

Angela Anderson, 13

Kalu

Black is Anthony, the person who is talking now.
Black is beautiful, like everyone here.
Black is a color that no one understands.
Black is cold like when you shiver in the snow.
Black is someone like you and me.
Black can fly like a bird in the sky.
Black is shiny like the sun upon us.
Black is a flower.
Black is Anthony, the one who finished the poem.

Anthony Miller, 12

A Poem Is the World

A poem is Native Americans dancing.
A poem is the sky
    and fish swimming.
A poem is a sunset
    that is very orange.
A poem is an old tree
who lives for many years.

A poem is people walking
    with deer around them.
A poem is like a jungle.
A poem is a man who is sad
because a tree fell down and died.

A poem is a face.

A poem is people searching
the trash for food.

A poem is children on the street
poor and homeless.

A poem is the world.

          Rosmery Ramirez, 16

WritersCorps History

Since its inception in 1994, WritersCorps has helped more than 40,000 people in some of America's most economically disadvantaged neighborhoods improve their literacy and self-sufficiency. WritersCorps has transformed the lives of thousands of youth at risk by teaching creative writing, giving voice to young people whose voices have been systematically ignored or disregarded. With its national readings and award-winning publications, WritersCorps has become a national arts and literacy model.

WritersCorps was born out of discussions between Jane Alexander, former Chairman of the National Endowment for the Arts (NEA), and Eli Siegel, then-director of AmeriCorps. Today, hundreds of writers have committed to teach in their communities, inspire youth, and work diligently to create a safe place for young people to write and discover themselves in the process. WritersCorps teachers make lasting connections with their community and become valued mentors and role models.

San Francisco, Washington, D.C. and Bronx, N.Y. were selected as the three initial sites for WritersCorps, chosen for their cities' exemplary art agencies with deep community roots and traditions of community activism among writers. In these three cities, WritersCorps' established writers, working at public schools and social service organizations, have helped people of virtually every race, ethnicity and age improve literacy and communication skills, while offering creative expression as an alternative to violence, alcohol and drug abuse.

In 1997, WritersCorps transitioned from a federally funded program to an independent alliance, supported by a collaboration of public and private partners. DC WritersCorps, Inc. is now a non-profit organization while the San Francisco and Bronx WritersCorps are projects of the San Francisco Arts Commission and Bronx Council for the Arts, respectively. WritersCorps has developed a national structure administered by the three sites to provide greater cooperation and visibility, while at the same time allowing the independence for each site to respond most effectively to its communities.

To learn more about WritersCorps contact:

Bronx WritersCorps
718-409-1265
www.bronxarts.org/aboutbca_programs.asp

DC WritersCorps
202-462-2885
www.dcwriterscorps.org

San Francisco WritersCorps
415-252-4655
www.writerscorps-sf.org

Aunt Lute Books is a multicultural women's press that has been committed to publishing high quality, culturally diverse literature since 1982. In 1990, the Aunt Lute Foundation was formed as a non-profit corporation to publish and distribute books that reflect the complex truths of women's lives and the possibilities for personal and social change. We seek work that explores the specificities of the very different histories from which we come, and that examines the intersections between the borders we all inhabit.

Please write, phone, or e-mail (books@auntlute.com) us if you would like to receive a free catalog of our books or if you wish to be on our mailing list for news of future titles. You may buy books from our website, by phoning in a credit card order, or by mailing a check with the catalog order form.

Aunt Lute Books
P.O. Box 410687
San Francisco, CA 94141
415.826.1300
www.auntlute.com